A CONCISE ACCOUNT OF NORTH AMERICA

1765

Originally Published in 1765 by
Major Robert Rogers

WITH
PREFACE AND APPENDIX
BY HIS FIFTH GREAT NEPHEW
William Michael Gorman

HERITAGE BOOKS
2007

HERITAGE BOOKS
AN IMPRINT OF HERITAGE BOOKS, INC.

Books, CDs, and more—Worldwide

For our listing of thousands of titles see our website at
www.HeritageBooks.com

Published 2007 by
HERITAGE BOOKS, INC.
Publishing Division
65 East Main Street
Westminster, Maryland 21157-5026

Copyright © 2007 William Michael Gorman

All rights reserved. No part of this book may be reproduced or transmitted in any form or by any means, electronic or mechanical, including photocopying, recording or by any information storage and retrieval system without written permission from the author, except for the inclusion of brief quotations in a review.

International Standard Book Number: 978-0-7884-4281-0

Dedication

Dedicated to my Great Great Grandparents

Mary Allen Rogers

and

Christopher Darius Gorman,

last of the great pioneers of my family.

Photo Courtesy: My cousin Joane Gardner

Contents

Preface	I
Original Cover Page	III
Introduction	V
North America	1
Newfoundland	3
Cape Breton	7
St. John's Island	9
Acadia or Nova Scotia	11
Province of Québec	19
New England	25
Province of Massachusetts Bay	31
Province of New Hampshire	37
Colony of Connecticut	41
Colony of Rhode Island	43
Province of New York	47
Province of New Jersey	55
Province of Pennsylvania	61
Maryland	67
Virginia	71
North & South Carolina & Georgia	93
North Carolina	99
South Carolina	101
Province of Georgia	105
East & West Florida	109
East Florida	109
West Florida	110
The Interior Country	113
River St. Lawrence & Great Lakes	115
Lake Huron	119
Lake Michigan	120
Green Bay	121
Lake Erie	124
Niagara Falls	126
Lake Ontario	128

Contents

River Christino	135
The Mississippi	141
Missouri River	144
Ohio River	145
Wabash River	146
Customs and Manners of the Indians	151
Appendix	187
Map	202

Preface

In honor of my 5th Great Granduncle, Colonel Robert Rogers, who was unfairly criticized and falsely villainized in his time. It is my wish to bring to light and honor his valiant and honorable efforts, which highly contributed the founding and establishment of the United States and Canada. Were it not for this great man, it is likely that New England, the United States west of the Rocky Mountains and Canada would now be a French territory and the Southwest United States would still be a part of Mexico.

Thomas Jefferson had a copy of Rogers' Concise Account of North America and sent Lewis and Clark on their famous expedition, following the Missouri River as Rogers had claimed would lead to the Shining Mountains and Oregon River, which flowed to the Pacific Ocean.

During the French & Indian War, Robert Rogers and his Rogers' Rangers led America's first war on terror and freed the colonists from the Abenakis of St. Francis, who were responsible for the destruction of his family's home in 1748 along with the murder, torture and kidnapping of over 600 colonist, who's scalps were found on poles throughout the village of St. Francis. This was the basis of Kenneth Roberts' novel and the movie staring Spencer Tracy, 'Northwest Passage'. In Roberts' book he repeatedly mentions Rogers' book 'A Concise Account of North America'.

Robert was offered command of the Continental Army before Washington, he turned down the offer likely because he wished to retire from military life to pursue other financial ventures as a private citizen. Later when he realized a military career was the only option he had Washington refused to let him join the Continentals because Washington claimed he was a British spy, when the truth is more likely Washington feared he might lose his command to the more popular Rogers. After being denied a position in

II

the Continental Army apparently Robert took a bit of retaliation on Washington by capturing the first American spy, Nathan Hale.

The U.S. Army's Rangers, Green Berets and other modern elite military units still employ tactics and standing orders developed by Robert Rogers. Also the U.S. Navy ships bearing the name "Ranger" were named for him and his colonial military units.

Following this preface, I have modernized the text and corrected spelling for the ease of the reader. In the appendix following the reprint will be notes of these corrections with the original spelling and explanations of text corrections.

A CONCISE ACCOUNT OF NORTH AMERICA

CONTAINING

A Description of the several British Colonies on that Continent, including the Islands of Newfoundland, Cape Breton, &c.

As To

Their Situation, Extent, Climate, Soil, Produce, Rise, Government, Religion, Present Boundaries, and the Number of Inhabitants supposed to be in each.

Also Of

The interior, or Westerly Parts of the Country, upon the Rivers St. Lawrence, the Mississippi, Christino, and the Great Lakes.
To which is subjoined,

An Account of the several Nations and Tribes of Indians residing in those Parts, as to their Customs, Manners, Government, Numbers, &c.

Containing many useful and entertaining facts never before treated of.

By Major ROBERT ROGERS.

L O N D O N:
Printed for the AUTHOR,
And sold by J. Millan, Bookseller, near Whitehall,
MDCCLXV

IV

Major Robert Rogers

November 7, 1731 ⸻ May 18, 1795

INTRODUCTION.

THE British Empire in North America is become so extensive and considerable, that it is presumed any attempts to transmit a just notion of it to the public will be favorably received by every Englishman who wishes well to his country; for, without a right knowledge of a country, new and unsettled, as a great part of this is, so distant from the feat of empire, it is not likely that, attention will be paid to the defending and peopling it, and to the encouraging commerce in it, which is indispensably requisite to render it advantageous to the nation in general, as well as to those individuals who become adventurers in it.

It will not be expected, after volumes upon volumes that have been published concerning the British colonies on the eastern shore of the American Continent that anything materially new can be related of them. The only thing I mean to attempt with regard to this is, to collect such facts and circumstances as in a political and commercial view, appear to me to be most interesting; to reduce them to an easy and familiar method, and contract them within such narrow limits, that the whole may be seen as it were at once, and everything material be collected from a few pages concerning seventeen provinces; a minute and circumstantial account of which would fill so many considerable volumes.

In doing this where my own knowledge (acquired by traveling several times thro' most of them) did not serve me, I have endeavored to make use of the most authentic materials collected from others, and to set every fact and circumstance in a true and impartial light, without favor or prejudice to any particular part or party.
But the principal object I have had in view, and what I look upon to be the most interesting and deserving part of this

VI

work, is the account I have given of the interior parts of North America, which though concise, and vastly short of what I should be glad to exhibit, I flatter myself is as full and perfect as any at present to be come at. Certain I am, that no one man besides has traveled over and seen so much as I have done and if my remarks and observations relative thereto are injudicious or wrongly placed, it is not owing to any want of attention to the subject, but merely to a want of skill. What is comprehended under the appellation of the Interior country of America is of itself, a larger territory than all the continent of Europe, and is at present mostly a desert, uninhabited except by savages; it cannot therefore be reasonably expected that one man has it in his power to give a just and minute account of its several parts, but that he must pass over large tracks of country in very general terms and in many things depend upon the reports of others, or proceed upon his own uncertain conjectures.

This wide-extended country may naturally enough be considered under three great rivers that take their rise near the center of it, namely, St. Lawrence, the Christino, and the Mississippi. The first of these I have traced, and am pretty well acquainted with the country adjacent to it as far up as Lake Superior, and with the country from the Green Bay westward to the Mississippi, and from thence down to the mouth of the Mississippi at the gulf of Mexico. I have also traveled the country adjacent to the Ohio and its principal branches, and that between the Ohio and the Lakes Erie and Michigan, add the countries of the southern Indians. But as to the country above Lake Superior, I have my intelligence chiefly from Indians, or from prisoners that have traveled with them into it. The same is the case as to the country at the head of the Mississippi, and that adjacent to the river Missouri. The Christino I have taken wholly from the Indians and though the accounts they have given me of these countries are large, and in some particulars very inviting, yet I shall do little more than mention their names, till I have better authority to go upon.

VII

In the account I have subjoined of the Indians, their customs, manners, &c. I have purposely omitted many things related by others who have wrote on that subject; some, because they are false, and others, because they are trite and trifling; and have only mentioned such as I thought most distinguishing, and absolutely necessary to give a just idea of the genius and policy of that people, and of the method in which they are to be treated. In order to our having any safe and advantageous commerce with them. And, without vanity, I may say, that the long and particular acquaintance I have had with several tribes and nations both in peace and war, has at least furnished me materials to treat the subject with propriety, however I may have failed in other respects. But I am not going to apologize or beg mercy at the hands of the critical, for it is far from being my ambition to shine as a learned and accurate historian; the only thing I mean to do is, in a simple and intelligible manner, to relate such matters of fact as may be useful to my country, and shall without any regret resign the plume to any one who performs the talk with greater life and ornament, and in a manner more pleasing to the public.

A Concise Account

OF

North America

AMERICA is divided into North and South, joining at the Isthmus of Darien. North America, to which my observations will be at present confined, lies between the latitude of 10 and 80 degrees north, and chiefly between the longitudes of 48 and 130 degrees west from the meridian of London, and is four thousand two hundred miles from the North to South, and about five thousand from East to West; being bounded on the East by the Atlantic ocean; by the gulf of Mexico, on the South; on the West by the Pacific Ocean; and by the Northern continent and ocean to the northward, through which, some suppose, there is a passage into the Pacific or Western ocean. A great part of this vast extent of territory is at present possessed by the subjects of his Britannic majesty, and the original natives or Indians, the number of which far exceeds that of the English. And that I may preserve some order and method, while I attempt a description of this country (so far as I have been able by my own travels and observations, and the information of others, to attain to the knowledge of it) I propose,

First, to describe the several British governments and colonies on the continent (including also the islands of Newfoundland, Cape Breton, and St. John's) separately; beginning with the northernmost, and traveling to the southward; in which the reader may expect a brief account of the rise, present extent and boundaries of those provinces; the number; of English inhabitants supposed to be in each; the climate, soil, commodities, government, religion, &c.

And, secondly, some account of the interior or western part of the country, so far as discoveries have been made, and of the Indian nations tribes that are known to us who inhabit it; as to their situation, numbers, manners, customs, and the connections and alliances that they have with each other, and with the English and French, &c.

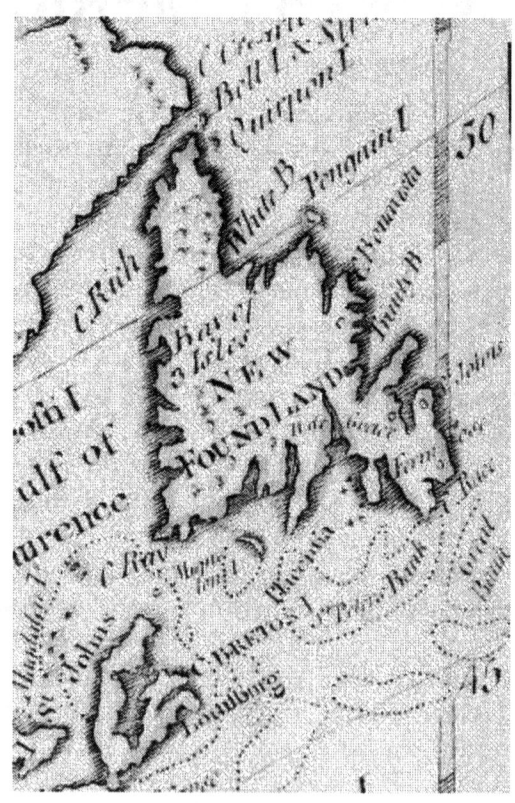

NEWFOUNDLAND

SO named by the first discoverer, is the most considerable island in North America for its extent, being situated east of the Gulf of St. Lawrence, between 46, 40 and 42 deg. 7 min. north latitude, and 41, 52 and 57 deg. 40 min. west longitude, is bound easterly and southerly by the Atlantic Ocean, northerly by the straights of Belle Isle, and on the west by the Gulf of St. Lawrence.

This island was discovered by the Cabots in 1497, who took possession of it in the name of King Henry VII.; but no colony was planted there till some considerable time after. This soil being not the most fertile, and the cold extremely severe, were circumstances, no doubt, which prevented the English from attempting a settlement here, till some time in the reign of Henry VIII, when they were allured to it, for the sake of fishing on the banks which lie off the south-easterly part of it.

In the reign of Queen Elizabeth, Sir William Gilbert was sent out with a commission, to prohibit all persons, not being her subjects, to fish upon the coast of this island. No land in the island were granted till 1610, when King James gave a grant to the Earl of Southampton, and others, of all that part of Newfoundland, lying between Cape Bona Vista and Cape St. Mary. Some Bristol merchants being joined in the patent; the settlement took the name of the Bristol Plantation. Sir George Calvert purchased some lands of this company, upon the southeast coast, sent thither a colony, and afterward, followed himself, and erected some houses and a fort. But being afterwards created Lord Baltimore, and getting a grant of Maryland, he abandoned the frozen coasts of Newfoundland and began the settlement of that province.

During the protectorship of Cromwell, Sir David Kirk, but without any commission, took possession of this island, where he lived and died; after which the original proprietors dropped their project of a settlement here, and the settlers that remained lived without any legal government. The French took advantage of this situation of things, and not only sent their ships to fish upon the coast, but erected a regular fort at Placentia, garrisoned at the expense of the government, and claimed the sole right to the island and fishery.

It continued in this posture during the reigns of Charles and James II, but, soon after the revolution, the British government renewed their ancient claim, and attempted to exclude the French from both the island and fishery, by the destruction of their fort at Placentia, which however at that time proved abortive.

The next summer Sir John Norris was sent with a squadron and 1500 land forces, with which he raised a regular fort at St. John's and leaving a garrison, returned to England, without attempting anything against the French. An Act of parliament was however passed, that no foreigner should fish on any of the rivers, lakes or coasts of Newfoundland ; but this proved a poor bulwark against the French, who, in 1705 laid siege to, and demolished the town of St. John's, with all the fishing stages, &c, but could not reduce the fort.

By the Treaty of Utrecht the island was again surrendered to the English, but they did not enjoy that and the fishery on the coasts, without repeated interruptions from the French; and in 1762 they took our fort at St. John's and reduced this island to their obedience; but, by the vigilance and activity of British commanders and troops then in America, were dispossessed of it the same summer, after they had considerably improved our fortifications there, and are at this time entirely excluded from the island and the fishery on the coasts, except on the island bank, and a few small islands that lie off between Cape Ray and Cape St. Mary.

The soil of this island, as hath been hinted, is very barren (excepting some glades upon the banks of rivers) in the island parts of it, rising into hills, or sinking into bogs and swamps, and where not covered with water, affords nothing but shrubs, spruce, and white moss.

There are in this island many fine rivers, lakes, and rivulets, which abound with beaver, otters and the like, and in which is great plenty of salmon, and many other kinds of fish. There is also great plenty of wild fowl, and the forests are stored with deer, moose, bears, and wolves, in great plenty. But the great and staple commodity of this island is cod fish, which are here larger and in greater abundance than in any part of the world is at percent supplied with this article chiefly from hence.

There are annually employed from Great Britain and North America, at the lowest computation, upwards of three hundred sail of vessels in the fishing business; on board of which, and on shore, to manufacture the fish, are not less than 10,000 hands; so that it is at the same time a very profitable branch of trade to the merchant, a source of livelihood to so many thousands of poor people, and a most excellent nursery to the royal navy, which is hence supplied with great numbers of able men. There are also taken, in great abundance on there coasts, mackerel, whales, seals, porpoises, &c. so that above 5,000 barrels of oil, besides a great quantity of whalebone, seal skins, &c. are annually reported from hence to different parts of the world, which may sufficiently point out the importance of the island, notwithstanding the roughness and barrenness of soil, and severity of the climate.

The numbers of English inhabitants on this island is uncertain and being near double the number in summer to what there is in the winter.

St. John's, situated on the southerly part of the island, is the capital town, containing between three and fourscore houses.

These coasts are observed to be extremely subject to fogs, occasioned by the vapors, which are exhaled from the lakes, swamps and bogs, with which the island abounds, as is generally supposed; but perhaps is more owing to the vast shoals of fish and sea animals which frequent these coasts, whose breath, warmth, and motion, occasion vapors to rise from the sea; hence I imagine it is, that, notwithstanding the almost perpetual fogs here, the air is wholesome and agreeable to most constitutions, which would hardly be the case if they sprung from bogs, swamps, and fresh water lakes.

The winters are severe, attended with almost continual storms of snow, sleet, &c, the sky being generally overcast.

Here are few cattle, sheep, or horses; instead of the latter, the inhabitants make use of dogs for drawing of wood and other conveyances, which they manage with great dexterity, fixing them in leather collars, to any number they please.

The government of this island is at present vested in the crown of Great Britain, including with it the islands of Anticosti and Madelaine, and others of smaller note, and the coasts of Labrador, from the river St. John's to Hudson's straights.

The religion professed by the inhabitants is that of the established Church of England.

CAPE BRETON

THIS island is situated to the southwest of Newfoundland, in 46 deg. north latitude, and 58 deg. 30 min. west longitude; distant from Newfoundland about 15 leagues, and separated from the continent by a narrow passage on the west. Its length is about 110 miles from north-east to south-west, and about 66 wide.

The soil and climate here are very much the same as in Newfoundland, and consequently its produce is not greatly different.

There have been discovered in its mountains, some coal mines, which, it is thought, may be worked to great advantage.

There are several harbours and bays round the island, and by its situation in the Gulf of St. Lawrence, may be looked upon as the key of Canada, being a safe retreat for ships bound either to or from thence.

This together with its conveniency for fishing, inducing the French, when they were excluded from Newfoundland and Acadia, to begin a settlement here in 1714, which they continued to increase, and in 1720, erected a fortification; they were, however, dispossessed in 1745 by New Englanders, and troops under the command of Sir William Pepperell, with the assistance of some men of war, Commodore, afterwards Sir Peter Warren. It was again ceded to the French by the treaty of Aix-la-Chapelle, who spared no pains or expense to strengthen it till 1758, when it was again reduced by British troops, Gen. Amherst commanding by land, and Admiral Boscawen by sea. Since the conquest of all Canada, the fortifications, by orders from the crown of Great Britain, have been blown up, and the town dismantled.

The port of Louisburg is a league in length, and a quarter of a league broad, with good anchoring ground, from six to ten fathom water. The harbour is generally froze from November till May.

There are several other harbours round this island, the most considerable of which is Port Thoulouse, where are more inhabitants than at Louisburg, from which it is distant eighteen leagues.

This Island is at present under the jurisdiction of the Governor of Nova Scotia.

St. John's Island

THIS Island, tho' situated in the neighborhood of Cape Breton, being partly between that and the continent, and consequently has no great difference in climate, yet varies widely from it as to the pleasantness and fertility of its soil. It is computed to be about fifty miles in length, has a commodious harbour, and great conveniences for carrying on the fishery. It abounds with variety of useful timber, and most kinds of wild game common to the country.

In the rivers (of which there are several) is plenty of salmon, trout, eels. &c. The surrounding sea abounds with sturgeon, plaice, and most kinds of shell fish. In short, so fertile is this island, being so well improved while possessed by the French, that it was justly styled the granny of Canada, furnishing them in great abundance with most kinds of grain, as well as great quantities of beef, pork, &c.

This island was settled by French about the same time as Cape Breton, and (excepting that it was not given up when reduced by Sir William Pepperel) has undergone the same revolutions with it; for tho' it was in some degree (while possessed by the French) a distinct separate government, yet the commander was subordinate to the Governor of Cape Breton, from whom he received his orders; and in the last reduction of Cape Breton, this island was included in the capitalization, and was surrendered to Lieutenant Colonel Rollo, when he found upon it 4,000 inhabitants, and upwards of 10,000 head of live cattle; and, what was shocking, found in the Governor's house several English scalps, which were brought there to market by savages of Nova Scotia, this being the place where they were supplied and encouraged to carry on their inhuman trade.

10 A CONCISE ACCOUNT OF

There are yet considerable quantities of land uncultivated on this island, which, when improved, will render it still more valuable.

This Island, at present, is under the Government of Nova Scotia, as are the lesser islands adjacent.

ACADIA, or NOVA SCOTIA

THIS part of the continent of North America is situated between 44 and 49 degrees north latitude, and is bounded southerly by the Atlantic Ocean; westerly by the Bay of Fundy, and the province of Maine, belonging to the Massachuset's Bay; northerly by Canada or the province of Quebec; and easterly by the Gulf of St. Lawrence.

Tho' this country was discovered by Sebastian Cabot in 1497, yet it lay neglected many years, and underwent several changes and renovations before any considerable settlement was made on it.

In 1758, Sir Humphrey Gilbert obtained a grant from Queen Elizabeth of all remote lands he should discover and settle. He set out, with a view to this part of America among others; but being lost on the coast of the continent, the project dropt.

In 1621, King James gave a grant of this province to Sir William Alexander, afterwards Earl of Stirling, and Secretary of State for Scotland, by whom it was called Nova Scotia. The French, in the mean time, had attempted some settlements in this territory; but were disturbed therein by Governor of Virginia, who sent Captain Argal to remove them in 1614, which was accordingly done.

In 1622, a ship was sent out by Sir William, with a number of people, and all kinds of necessaries for beginning a settlement. These people landed near Cape Sable; but I cannot find, after all, that they made any settlement. It is however certain that some of our people were settled here in 1631; for, in 1632, Quebec and Cape Breton, which had been taken from the French, together with this province, were ceded to them again by the treaty between Charles I and Lewis XIII, when a number of English removed out of it till 1654, when Oliver Cromwell sent Major Sedgwick, who took Port Royal, and obliged the French to quit the country of Nova Scotia. It continued in our possession till the reign of Charles II. When it was again ceded to the French by the Treaty of Breda, who kept it undisturbed till 1690, when the New England people finding it inconvenient to have the French so near them, prepared a fleet, and a proper number of land forces, and gave the command to sir William Phips, a native of that province, who sailing from New England the 28th April 1690, arrived before Port Royal, now Annapolis, in May following, which he quickly reduced, obliging the inhabitants there to submit to the English government, or be transported to Canada. Most of them, for the sake of keeping their estates and habitations, consented to become British subjects, but very soon began to act as enemies or at least very bad neighbors to the people of New England.

In 1710, her Majesty Queen Anne, listening to their repeated complaints and solicitations, sent a squadron and some land forces under Colonel Nicholson, who took Port Royal, and, in honour to the Queen, called it Annapolis, bringing the whole country into subjection; and at the Treaty of Utecht it was absolutely yielded to Great Britain, by an express article in that treaty. Those of the inhabitants, who chose to remain, were to become British subjects, and enjoy their religion so far as the laws of Great Britain would admit. And in order to secure their obedience, and to keep possession of the country, a garrison was kept at Port Royal, and another small one at Canso; but still no government was established, nor any suitable encouragement given to our people to settle there; so that things naturally dwindling, the inhabitants, in spite of their oaths of allegiance, soon began to consider themselves as French subjects again; and accordingly, in 1744, assisted a parcel of French in the reduction of the fort at Canso, and made an attempt upon Annapolis; but without success, that garrison being seasonably relieved from New England. They continued to commit hostilities themselves, at least secretly, and to supply and encourage the eastern Indians to perpetrate the most horrid acts of cruelty and barbarity on the English on the frontiers of New England, whose scalps or persons were carried to market in Louisburg, Québec, &c. (not only in time of war, but of peace), and there exchanged for powder, ball, or what ever they wanted. Nor was an entire stop put to these practices * till the beginning of the last war, when being convinced that these French rebels (called neutrals, on account of their having been sworn to allegiance to the crown of Great Britain) were more inveterate and dangerous enemies than those who were under no such obligation; and finding that every other method to reconcile them to the British government was ineffectual, they were by force deprived of their estates, and with their families totally rooted out of the province, and scattered through the other British colonies on the continent.

On the sea coasts of this province are many safe and convenient harbours; but none equal to that of Chebucta, or Halifax, which is allowed to be the finest in America, and capable of being made equal to any in Europe, both for safety and conveniency, having good anchoring ground, and water sufficient for any ship that swims. It is the place of rendezvous for the Royal dock, and conveniences for a ship of any rate, to have down and careen; for which end it is resorted to by his Majesty's ships, from all parts of America and the West Indies.

These people in 1754, when the Duke d'Anville with a considerable force, came to establish a garrison and settlement at Chebucta, assembled, with a number of Indians, to assist him; and about that time cut off Colonel Noble, with his whole party, at Menis, where he was posted, to keep them in subjection.

Situated on the west side of this harbour is the town Halifax, which tho' its foundations were laid in 1747, is now a considerable town, consisting of upwards of a thousand houses, and is the capital of the whole province; and indeed, from the same era we may date the origin of this province, there being no government properly established in it till then.

There are also several other towns laid out round this bay, and partly inhabited; but the most considerable settlements ate upon the rivers which fall into it.

The inhabitants in this province may be computed at about twenty thousand. Its northerly situation exposes it to severe cold and deep snows in winter; but is generally very healthy, and agreeable to English constitutions, as are all the northern provinces. The soil of this province is various, being in some parts very rough and barren; in others exceeding pleasant and fertile, as it is in particular round the Bay of Fundy, and on the afore mentioned rivers, which fall into it, where are large tracts of marsh that extend on the sides of these rivers for fifty or sixty miles into the country, and several miles from the bay, which, being dyked, is improved to great advantage. The upland in this province is likewise very pleasant and fruitful, producing wheat, rye, Indian corn, peas, beans, hemp, flax, &c. and some kind of northerly fruit, to great perfection. The rivers abound with salmon and other kinds of river fish, common to the coast; and several fisheries are erected in different harbours here, which are carried on with good success; nor is it inferior to any of the northern provinces in respect to wild beasts and fowls.

The commodities exported from this province to other parts are chiefly lumber, such as plank, staves, hoops, joints, &c. and fish.

ACADIA or NOVA SCOTIA

There is great mixture of religious professions here; there being some of the Church of England, others Presbyterians, Congregationalists, Baptists, &c.

The King is Sovereign of the soil, and appoints the Governor, who is his Captain General; the Lieutenant Governor and Council are likewise appointed by his Majesty, which form the upper house, and the lower house is formed of the representatives, who are chosen by freeholders; but the Governor can negative their choice.

As fishing is the staple commodity, and almost the only article of trade in the provinces of Newfoundland and Nova Scotia, with their dependant islands; and there are the only places in America where trade is carried on to say perfection, it will not perhaps, be disagreeable to the reader to give some account in this place of the method which they take to cure and manufacture the cod fish fit for market.

The fish caught near the shore are observed to be by far the best; the vessels employed in this business are generally small shallops*, which come to shore every day, where the fishermen throw the cod upon a stage prepared for that purpose. One of them, who is called the Beheader, opens the fish with a two edge knife, and cuts off his head; a second hands the fish on to the carver, who stands opposite him at a table erected upon the stage; the carver with a single edge knife, six or eight inches long, and very thick on the back to increase its weight, splits the fish open; then it is conveyed to the Salter, who places it with the skin undermost in a barrel, and then very slightly covers it with salt, laying the fish regularly upon one another. After leaving the cod in salt three or four days, and sometimes double that time and longer, according to the season, they put it into a tub, and wash it well,

* *Shallops were small boats.*

afterwards they make it up in piles, and in fair weather spread it out, with the skin undermost, on a kind of stage raised with wattles, about two feet from the ground, or upon stones; before night they turn the skin uppermost, which they also do whenever it rains; when the fish has been dried a little, it is raised into larger piles, where it rests a day or two; after which it is again exposed to the air, and turned according as there is occasion, before they raise it into larger piles in the same form, where, after this operation, it sometimes remains fifteen days without being moved at all; at the end of which it is once more exposed to the air, and, when almost dry, gathered together again, in order to sweat; which operation takes twenty four hours or more, according to the season; then it is opened the last time to the sky, and, when thoroughly dry, housed.

Fish manufactured in this manner are not only more fair to the eye, but more grateful to the taste, than those that are partly prepared at sea; as is the case with larger vessels which go out, and are loaded, before they return, opening, salting, and packing their fish in the vessel's hold, by which means it is forty or fifty days, and often much longer, before the necessary operation, to render the fish good and agreeable, can be attended to. When they return to shore, they proceed with it as before mentioned.

The fish cured in the spring is generally the best, if properly prepared; which depends on the skill and diligence of those employed about it, and also upon the quality of the salt made use of; on which last account, the English caught fish is generally inferior to the American, the salt they make use of often having a mineral quality, or perhaps it may be as much owing to their not having the like opportunity to prepare it seasonably, by reason of the length of the voyage.

The fish caught in October or November may continue in salt till March, or the beginning of April, without any sensible damage, when it is washed, and undergoes the process above described.

the PROVINCE of QUEBEC

THIS province is much the largest of any upon the continent. QUEBEC, which is the metropolis, and near the center of it, is situated in 46 deg. 55 min. north latitude, and 69 deg. 48 min. west longitude; and is bound northeasterly by the Gulf of St. Lawrence, and the river St. John's; northwesterly by wild uninhabited lands; southwesterly by the same; and southerly, by the province of New York, the New England provinces, and the province of Nova Scotia; extending from northeast to southwest about five hundred miles, and is upwards of two hundred miles wide. This country was first settled by French, who kept the possession and government of it till September 13, 1759, when Québec was surrendered to the Generals Monckton and Townshend, commanding the British troops that had been destined for expedition against it the preceding spring, under the command of General Wolfe; and September 1760 all Canada was given up to the English in the capitulation at Montreal, agree upon and signed by General Amherst, and Monsieur de Vaudreueil the French Governor, and has since been confirmed to the British crown by the Treaty of Fontainebleau. The French comprehended under the name of Canada a much larger territory than the above mentioned, taking into their claim great part of the New England provinces, and of the provinces of New York and Nova Scotia, and northerly to Hudson's Bay, and westerly to the Pacific Ocean, and southerly to the Gulf of Mexico; and had erected a chain of forts, from the north of the river St. Lawrence to their settlements at Louisiana, to support their claim.

They began the settlement of this province in 1605 in Québec, situated on the north shore of the river St.

Lawrence, about three hundred miles from the mouth; and about the same time settlements were begun upon the island of Orleans, which is in the river, a little below Québec, and on each side of the river to the mouth of it, and several smaller rivers that fall into it. Up the river, from Québec about twenty miles, they soon after began a settlement called Jecorty, and erected a fort at Chamblee, on the river Sorriel, near where it falls out of Lake Champlain. Soon after this, the foundations of Montreal were laid on the island of Montreal, situated in the river St. Lawrence, about 200 miles above Quebec.

Another considerable settlement was made at Trois Rivieres, or the Three Rivers, so called from a river's disemboguing itself by three mouths or channels into the River St. Lawrence; and is situated about halfway between Québec and Montreal, in a very delightful place, affording a prospect the most agreeable to the eye of any in the whole country. There are many other settlements upon the banks of the River St. Lawrence, and of those which empty into it, as well as islands surrounded by it; but none deserving of particular notice in the place, except Québec and Montreal, already mentioned. The former contains upwards of 1,500 dwelling houses, well built, besides several public buildings, which are stately and splendid, and were built for different uses, some by charitable persons, and others by the government of France; there are among these several hospitals, and not far from the town without the walls was a nunnery very well built, as was the mansion house of their Bishop and Jesuits. This Town, besides the natural safety of its situation is now well fortified. Montreal is near as large and populous as Québec, and is much more pleasantly situated. The streets are regular, the houses well built, commodious and agreeable; and you may see every house at one view from the harbour; or from the southernmost side of the river, as the hill, on the side of which the town stands falls gradually into the waters. The public buildings here exceed those of Québec for beauty, and are equal in number,

The PROVINCE of QUEBEC 21

excepting the Bishops palace and the cathedral church. The number of inhabitants in Canada is upwards of 100,000. The island of Montreal is exceedingly fertile, and well improved, producing great plenty of greens, and some fruit; but the island of Jesus, to the north of Montreal, is more level, and deemed better land. There are several other islands to the north, which are formed by the Attawawas River, and which are improved. This river forms also the island of Montreal, by one part at its entering at the west end of it into the Lake St. Francis; and the other part passing north of Montreal, forming the island of Jesus, and many other of smaller note, and joins St. Lawrence at the east end of the island of Montreal. About the center of this island are two mountains called the Twins, remarkable for being exactly alike; they are pretty high, and much to the beauty of the island. In the Lake St. Francis, southwest of Montreal, are several islands that are inhabited and well improved; St. Pierre is the most considerable of them. Their uppermost settlements in the province are at the Cedars, the westerly limits of the province, at the bottom of the falls from Lake Ontario.

The rivers branching thro' this extensive country are very numerous, and many of them navigable a considerable ways into the country; but they are all swallowed up in the river St. Lawrence. This river is eighty miles wide at its entrance into the sea at Cape Rosiers, on the side of Nova Scotia; something to the eastward of which is the island of Anticosti, of not much account. The course of the river is nearly through the middle of the province, from the southwest to a good many navigable rivers, and forming a great variety of bays, harbours, and islands; the most pleasant and fruitful of which is the island of Orleans, a little below Québec, producing in great abundance all kinds of grain and vegetables common to the climate. This island is twenty one miles in length, and three or four wide.

The French, while they had possession of this province, very industriously represented the navigation of the river

St. Lawrence to be difficult and dangerous; but we have since found the contrary to be the case, ships of the line meeting no difficulty in going to Québec. The land in general, on both sides of the river, is low and level; indeed opposite to Québec are two considerable mountains, called the Lady Mountains, which from this place run southwest through this continent to the country of the Creek Indians, at the north part of the Two Florida's in one continual ridge; and wherever rivers have forced their way through them, they rise on each side very steep to their common heights. This ridge of mountains is called the Appalachian Hills; and again at Montreal some hills appear to the northwest of it.

The climate here is cold, the winters long and tedious, especially in the northeasterly parts of the province; notwithstanding which the soil is none the worst, being in some parts both pleasant and fertile, productive of most kinds of English grain and vegetables, common to the climate, in great abundance; especially the island of Orleans already mentioned, and the islands and lands near it, which are remarkable for their rich and easy soil.

The summers in this country are exceedingly pleasant, and so prolific that the farmer expects to reap his crop in sixteen weeks from the sowing of his seed. There is in some parts of this province very excellent timber, such as white pines, oak of different kinds, and spruce in great abundance. And as the lakes and rivers are well stored with salmon, eels, and all kinds of fish common to such waters, so its forests are abound with deer, moose, bears, &c. There are also beavers, otters, martins, &c. in great plenty. In short notwithstanding its northwardly situation, it may be justly denominated a healthy, fruitful, and pleasant country, affording most of the necessaries and conveniences of life; having (tho' mostly situate within land) all the advantages of an extended sea coast, by means of the river St. Lawrence, which affords an easy conveyance from one part of the province to another, and a cheap importation of foreign commodities, even to the remotest parts of it.

The PROVINCE of QUEBEC 23

The chief commodities exported from this province are timber, furs, deer, elk, and moose skins, &c. The government of this province is the same as Nova Scotia.

The religion professed by the French inhabitants is that of the Church of Rome, they being tolerated in the free exercise of it by an article in the capitulation, which was confirmed to them by the subsequent treaty, his Britannic Majesty having the appointment of their Bishop. The English, residing here are of the Church of England.

NEW ENGLAND

THAT part of the continent of America called New England is situated between 41 and 43 degrees 50 min. north latitude, and 64 deg. 40 min. and 73 deg. west longitude, is bound northeasterly and easterly by Nova Scotia and the Bay of Fundy, northwesterly by Canada, westerly by the province of New York, southerly by the South, and northeasterly by the Atlantic Ocean, having its seacoast very irregular and broken by a variety of bays and inlets.

This territory is divided into five distinct districts or governments; the most northerly is the province of Main, which is now called the county of York, being under the jurisdiction of the Massachusetts Bay; next to this county and between it and the Massachusetts Bay, is New Hampshire; next to the bay government is the colony of Rhode Island; to the south and west of both of them is the colony of Connecticut. These several districts in effect, took their rise from the first settlement made by the English in this country, which was the colony of Plymouth, situated near Cape Cod, and which now, as well as the province of Maine, is incorporated into that of Massachusetts Bay.

The colony of Plymouth was begun by a number of adventures in 1621, who, for the sake of liberty they could not then enjoy in their native country, were persuaded to exchange it for this, at that time a hideous wilderness, whole only inhabitants were wild beasts, or men almost as wild and as savage as they. They sailed from Plymouth in England in the month of September, with an intention to begin a settlement at the mouth of Hudson's River, where they had made purchase of a tract of land of the company to whom those had been granted; but meeting with a storm they fell in the Cape Cod the November following, and finding here a safe harbour, they fixed upon a place for their present settlement, and called it Plymouth, from the place of their embarkation, which name it still retains.

It is not to be doubted but they suffered many hardships and inconveniencies at their first settlement, for want of accommodations not presently to be procured in this new world. They happened however to light on a part of the continent from which the savages had retired, on account of a war subsisting between two nations of them; so that they continued in quiet possession for a great number of years. Indeed the Indians in the neighborhood appeared disposed to peace and friendship, each of the contending parties perhaps hoping for assistance from new comers.

But the emigrants, not depending on the good disposition of their Heathen neighbors, quickly after their landing enclosed an old Indian field with palisades, and erected a fort, on which they planted some cannon to keep them in awe. The following spring they purchased a tract of land of one of the Indian chiefs. Having thus laid the foundation of their colony they proceeded to the choice of their first Governor for one year, and chose Mr. John Carver; but he dying before the year expired, was succeeded by William Bradford, Esq.; who was continued their Governor, by an annual election for several years.

This infant colony was annually reinforced by fresh adventurers from the mother country, so that by the year 1628 their numbers and improvements were considerable; and being not satisfied with their Indian title, they this year obtained a grant from the aforesaid company of this colony; and another for all the lands within three miles north of the Merrimack River, to three miles south of Charles River, where it falls into the sea at the bottom of the Massachusetts Bay. And the next year six ships, with 350 passengers, arrived at Salem, with a large stock of cattle of all sorts, and other necessaries.

The year following a still larger fleet arrived, by which the colony was so increased that they judged it most expedient to divide, from them removing and laying the foundation of a town called Boston, which for its conveniency and security is become the metropolis of New England. The first Governor of Boston or the Massachusetts colony was John Wenthrop, Esq.; Numbers continued to flock into these new colonies, induced to it either for the sake of religion or trade; and about this time some religious principles were broached by one Williams, a minister of Salem, for which he and his followers, refusing to recant, they were expelled the Massachusetts colony, and built a new town, which they called Providence, upon New Port River, near Rhode Island.

Hitherto those colonies had not been in the least molested by the savages; but this year a nation called the Pequots, who lived on the Connecticut River, committed some murders, for which they were not chastised by the English, upon their promise to deliver up the murderers, till some time afterwards, when they refused to fulfill their promise, and repeated their outrages upon the inhabitants of a village named Weathersfield upon the Connecticut River; for which they were severely punished by a company of 100 men, commanded by Captain Mason, who destroyed one of their forts, and near 400 of them, at one time.

In 1635, no less than twenty sail loaded with goods and passengers arrived at Boston, with them came Mr. Henry Vane, afterwards Sir Henry Vane, intending with these people to begin a. settlement on the Connecticut River, but being chose Governor the year ensuing for the Massachusetts he laid by the design of beginning a new colony for the present; but the next year, on some religious pretences, he being inclined to favor the Anabaptist, they left him out, and chose their old Governor Mr. Wenthrop. In 1636, on account of the behavior of The Pequot Indians before mentioned, it was thought expedient for the safety of both colonies, to make a settlement upon the Connecticut River, and towns were built accordingly on both sides of the river, at Hertford, and other places. But this being out of the limits of the other colonies, they formed themselves a separate government.

In 1637, on account of some ecclesiastical severities, then put in practice in England, a new fleet, with a great number of people, on board, and among others Dr. Davenport, who quitted his church in Coleman street London, arrived in New England. But finding no convenient place to settle in the Massachusetts, without retiring further into the country than they chose, they purchased from the Indians the lands lying on the sea coast, between the Connecticut River, and Hudson's River, where they built a town, naming it New Haven, from whence the colony derived the name of the New Haven Colony. And, whilst colonies were thus named settling to the southward, others, induced by the profits arising from the fur trade, settled themselves to the northeast between the rivers Merrimack and Kennebec, and formed two distinct colonies, one named New Hampshire, and the other (still further to the eastward) was called the Province of Maine.

One would have thought that a people who had so lately seen the sad consequences of religious disputes, especially when heightened into perfection, would have carefully avoided every appearance of that kind among themselves; but so it was, that, about this time there was a synod or convention of ministers, with their lay elders, or delegates of the churches, called, out of both colonies of Plymouth and the Massachusetts, by whom it was most solemnly decreed, that every person, holding to some particular opinions, should be banished out of those colonies.

This thundering sentence from the awful tribunal they had erected, instead of reconciling the minds of those it was aimed against, as is generally the case, rendered them more zealous and obstinate, and in the end gave rise to another distinct colony, for, banished from their countrymen, they purchased of the natives the island of Aquetnet, so called by

NEW ENGLAND

the Indians, and made a settlement there called the colony of Rhode Island.

Thus in the space of about fifteen years, the English emigrants had possession of this country, from the river Kennebeck on the northeast, almost to Hudson's River, southwest, an extent of upwards of 400 miles on the sea coast. Such was the first rise and origin of the New England colonies, which from these small beginnings are now become very considerable, and deserve a separate description, in which as their situation hath been already laid down, it is in no ways material in what order we take them.

the PROVINCE of MASSACHUSET'S BAY

THIS province at present contains what were formerly the colonies of Plymouth, Massachusetts Bay, and the Province of Maine the latter separated from the others by the province of New Hampshire, running in between them about 30 miles wide upon the sea. Indeed for several years the province of New Hampshire, as well as the scattering settlements of Nova Scotia, were under the jurisdiction of this province. That part of it called the Province of Maine, or county of York, is bounded westerly by New Hampshire, northerly by Nova Scotia, or the river St. Johns, southeasterly and southwardly by the sea for near 200 miles. The other part of this province has New Hampshire, for its northerly boundary, easterly and southerly by the sea, southwest and westerly by the colonies of Rhode Island and Connecticut, and the province of New York.

It would fill a volume itself to give a particular account of the various remarkable occurrences and revolutions that have happened in church and state within this province, from its origin to this time; I shall therefore only relate such as are the most distinguishing ones.

In 1684, for some political reforms, the colonies of Plymouth, the Massachusetts, and province of Maine, made a resignation of their charters into the hands of the then King, and, were thereupon incorporated into one province, but not with all the privileges they had before enjoyed, they having given reason to suspect, by some extraordinary proceedings they had been guilty of, that they would abuse their liberty (unbounded as it had been) into licentiousness, if indulging any longer. Mr. Cransfield was by King Charles appointed their first Governor, after this incorporation; and, after him, Joseph Dudley, Esquire, by King James; who pretty soon, tho' a native of New England, had the misfortune to be sent prisoner to England by his disaffected countrymen, who reassumed their old privileges of choosing their own magistrates. Such was the situation of things at this time in Great Britain, that this act of rebellion was in a sort winked at by the government.

Indeed Sir Edmund Andrews was sent over to be their Governor; but with instructions to confirm all subordinate magistrates agreeable to their choice. Sir Edmund kept his authority no longer than till the news of the Revolution arrived, when they once more assumed their ancient privilege, and elected a Governor and other magistrates of their own; which usurpation they maintained for some time, under countenance of a letter from King William and Queen Mary, dated August 12, 1689.

Having for a long time experienced the inconveniencies of this unsettled form of government, they petitioned for the restoration of their charter upon the former footing, which was refused them. They however obtained a new charter, by which the appointment of the Governor and several other prerogatives were refereed to the crown, allowing them to choose their first Governor; they accordingly made choice of Sir William Phips, who had presented their petition at home. Sir William arrived in May 1692, and took upon him the government of the Massachusetts and New Hampshire, agreeable to his Majesty's commission.

About this time a most shocking tragedy was acted in this province, several persons being accused, tried condemned, and executed, for witchcraft, and others imprisoned; but the next year they celebrated a public fast, to beg forgiveness of the Almighty for their having murdered the innocent the year before.

In 1741 (till which time nothing extraordinary happened) * William Shirley, Esq. was appointed Governor of this province, district from New Hampshire, of which Mr.

Wentworth had been appointed Governor the year before. Till this time the Governor of the Massachusetts Bay had also commissioned Governor of New Hampshire, and acted as such, either personally, or by his deputy.

The town of Boston is situated upon a peninsula at the bottom of Massachusetts Bay, and contains between 4 and 5000 houses, which in general are well built; and several of the public buildings are very spacious and elegant; there are in the town seventeen educes appropriated for public worship, a house where their council and assembly, and courts of justice, sit; another for the Governor's dense; and a spacious market, and a hall above it, called Fanniuel Hall, from Mr. Fanniuel, who was its generous founder. The number of inhabitants in the whole province is computed to be upwards of 20,000.

* *There were several Governors between Mr. Phips and Mr. Shirley, namely, Mess. Shout, Dummer, Belcher, &c. and Mr. Pownel, and Mr. Bernard, the present Governor.*

That part of the province called county of York has very old soil, great part of it towards the province of Québec, being mountainous, is entirely unfit for agriculture; and that towards the sea coasts is low, covered with spruce, and white and yellow pines, and some oaks, excepting near the banks of rivers, which fall from the mountains (of which there is a great number) on which multitudes of saw mills are erected. Here may be found plenty of oak, ash and maple; and on several of these rivers, for many miles together, the land is pretty good; and doubtless would have been better improved, had not the inhabitants for many years past kept in almost continual alarms, and sometimes driven from their plantations by the savages.

There are several safe and convenient harbours along the sea coasts, the principal of which is Casco Bay, the most considerable town in the country, where great part of the masts for the royal navy are in.

There are some few fisheries begun upon these coasts but are not yet become considerable. This part of the province is well stored with wild game, and from it are exported considerable quantities of furs and skins.

The other part of the province has a variety of soil, it being in some places very barren, in others fertile, and abundantly productive of Indian rye, oats, barley, flax, peas, &c. wheat being raised only in the westerly parts of it. The surface is generally rocky and uneven, excepting near the rivers, where are some pleasant intervals.

The timber natural to this soil is chiefly oak, white pine, maple, walnut and chestnut. The country abounds in fruit trees, such as apples, pears, peaches, plumbs and cherries of most kinds. The rivers are well stored with fish, and the neighboring sea affords a plenty of cod, mackerel and the like; to the banks of Newfoundland, Isle of Sable, &c. especially from the town of Marble-Head where is the most considerable fishery in New England.

The chief commodities exported from this province are ships ready built, timber, furs, fish, pot ash, cast iron ware, oil, tallow, &c.

His Britannic Majesty appoints the Governor, Lieutenant Governor, Secretary, and the officers of the Admiralty, in this province; and the freeholders choose a house of representatives, who choose a Speaker and Council, or upper house. The Governor, however, can negative their choice; but he and all the officers in the province (except the Comptroller of his Majesty's Customs) receive their salaries by vote of the two houses, who have never yet been brought to settle a salary not even upon the Governor, who generally has it in his instructions from his Majesty to insist upon their doing it. They however commonly grant him 1:001. Sterling per annum.

There are a number of churches in this province of the Episcopal persuasion; but by far the greater part are

the PROVINCE of MASSACHUSET'S BAY 35

Dissenters, upon the Congregational or Independent plan, having no ecclesiastical court that is authoritative or decisive; which, as I am told is a source of many inconveniencies to them, being the means of prolonging church quarrels and divisions among them.

It must however be said, that great care is taken of their education, free schools being established and supported by law, in most of their towns, which are generally supplied with able masters; and at Cambridge, about six miles from Boston, is a public seminary, or college, called Harvard, in which are annually graduated, bachelors and masters, from fifty to sixty young gentlemen.

the PROVINCE of
NEW HAMPSHIRE

THIS province is bounded on the south by Massachusetts Bay, on the west by New York, on the north by Canada, and northeasterly by the county of York, having at present only thirty miles of sea coast allowed to it.

The town Portsmouth, which is the metropolis of this province, contains about 700 dwelling houses, and four meeting houses and a chapel, is very pleasantly situated on Piscataqua Bay, having a safe and convenient harbour, where the largest ships may ride securely. From this port annually sail about 200 vessels, loaded chiefly with timber, fish, &c. for the West Indies, which having disposed of by sale or exchange, they reload, and proceed from thence to Europe, where both vessels and cargoes are sold, and the mariners return passengers.

The other considerable towns for trade in this province, are Hampton, Cochecha, and Exeter. Londonderry an inland town, about thirty five miles from Portsmouth, is considerable for manufacturing of linen, being peopled chiefly with the natives of Ireland.

The number of inhabitants in this province is about 70,000 which have greatly increased since the total reduction of Canada, settlements being in many new towns, where formerly they dared not attempt it, through fear of savages.

The soil of this province is various, much resembling that of the county of York already described, especially the northerly parts of it, being mountainous and broken.

The most considerable mountains in this province, and indeed in new England, are those called the White

Mountains, so called from their appearance, which is like snow, consisting, as is generally supposed, of white flint, from which the reflection of the sun is very brilliant and dazzling, and by their prodigious heights are to be seen at a very great distance, being often discovered by the seamen coasting the eastern shore, when all the intermediate land is entirely concealed. I cannot learn that any person was ever on the top of these mountains. I have been told by Indians that they have often attempted it in vain, by reason of the change of air they met with, which I am inclined to believe, having ascended them myself till the alteration of air was very perceptible, and even then I had not advanced half way up; the valleys below were then concealed from me by clouds. Indeed there are several other mountains in this country, whose tops are above the benefit of rain upon them.

The basis of the White Mountains is a tract of about fifty five miles square, from which they rise in cragged heads, one above the another, in an irregular manner, all the way to the top. For the first four or five miles, as you ascend them, you will find beach, hemlock, and some white pines; higher up the growth is chiefly black spruce for six or seven miles, where the sides are clad with a white moss; and if you advance still further, you will find scarce any thing growing; for which reason, if there was no other, the ascent would be very difficult, the mountain being extremely steep. There are many streams of water gushing out of the sides, which run down with great rapidity; indeed all the largest and best rivers in New England take their rise from some part of these mountains. Saco River rises from part of the south in several small riverlets, which in the course of a few miles join each other. This river runs through the county of York; on the banks of it are some fine intervals, which are annually overflowed when the snows melt, and thereby enriched. The riverlets breaking out from the southwest of the mountains, after various windings, fall into a lake called Winnipisiokee, out of which issues the river Merrimack, which, by the waters that join it, soon becomes a

the PROVINCE of NEW HAMPSHIRE

considerable stream. There are fine intervals upon it, overflowed and enriched like the former.

This river through the province of New Hampshire and part of Massachusetts, and has several towns or villages upon it pleasantly situated, but none so than a small one, in the province of New Hampshire, called Pennecock. From the north and west parts of the aforesaid mountains, Connecticut River takes its rise; the course of which is southerly, running across the provinces of New Hampshire, Massachusetts and Connecticut, till it empties itself into the sea or sound, between Connecticut and Long Island. This river, like the others, annually overflows its banks, and enriches the adjacent intervals, which in some places are very extensive, in each of the provinces it rolls through; but no where more so than at a place called the Cohas, in the province of New Hampshire, a tract of twenty miles in length, and six in breadth, which, for its beauty and fertility, may be deservedly styled the garden of New England.

The river Kennebeck, which is a considerable stream, likewise takes its rise at these mountains at the east, running thro' the county of York, and is endowed with the same properties as the former. There is also another river, rising from the north part of these mountains, which runs into the province of Québec, and falls into St. Lawrence, or St. Francis, and a part of the river Shedoir also rises at these mountains, and flows thro' the same province, till it joins the river St. Lawrence, twelve miles above Québec; by all which streams the riches of these hills, whose tops are inaccessible, are annually carried to and distributed among the neighboring provinces.

In the province of New Hampshire is a great plenty and variety of timber; its forests abound with all kinds of game common to the climate; and its rivers with salmon, shad, eels, trout, &c. Some fisheries are carried on in the sea ports, but its scanty limits on the sea forbid its becoming so considerable as its neighbors in that branch. The produce of the soil is chiefly Indian corn, rye, oats, peas, it being too cold for wheat; they also raise some hemp and flax, and breed black cattle, horses, sheep, &c. but in great abundance.

The chief commodities exported from this province, are, masts for the Royal Navy, staves, boards, shingles, furs, &c.

The Governor, Lieutenant Governor, Council, and Secretary, and the officers of the Admiralty in this province, are appointed by his Britannic Majesty, who is absolute sovereign of the soil. The several towns and districts choose their representatives; and all inferior executive officers are appointed by the Governor, with the advice of his Majesty's Council.

I cannot forbear mentioning here an inconvenience which this infant province labors under in judicial matters, namely, that there is but one place in the province at which the courts of justice are held, viz. at Portsmouth, one of the extremities, for which reason many of the inhabitants often have to travel 150 or 200 miles on trifling occasions.

The religion professed here is the same in general as in the adjoining province, there being but one Episcopal Church as yet erected, viz. in Portsmouth; and it is to be lamented that little pains or care is taken about the education of children, there being very few schools regularly kept up, or supplied with maters.

the COLONY of
CONNECTICUT

THIS colony comprehends what were originally the colony of Connecticut or Hartford, and that of New Haven, being incorporated into one in 1692, still retaining, by a charter then granted them, all the privileges of their ancient charter; and, indeed, ever since their union, they have kept up two seats of government, viz. Hartford and New Haven, at which places their general court of assembly sits alternately, for transacting the affairs of the colony. This colony is bounded by the Massachusetts on the north, New York on the west, southerly by the Sound, and easterly by Rhode Island and a part of the Massachusetts Bay. It has many fine towns, pleasantly situated upon the river Connecticut, and along the Sound; the principal of which, for trade and commerce, are New London, Hartford, and New Haven; the later of which situated on New Haven Bay, is elegantly laid out in regular streets, having a beautiful parade or common in the center; it contains about 200 dwelling houses, besides public buildings, among which is a college that has a very good appearance, and in which, I am told, learning flourishes; there being near a great number of young gentlemen annually graduated there as at Harvard in the Massachusetts.

The number of inhabitants in the whole colony is supposed to be about two hundred and ten thousand.

The soil of this country is various, much of it being uneven rocky, cold and barren; and other parts exceeding pleasant and fertile, especially on Connecticut River already mentioned, whose intervals produce all kinds of grain and fruit common to the climate in great abundance, rarely disappointing, and often exceeding the hopes of the husbandman. They also breed in this colony great numbers of black cattle, horses, and swine; make considerable proficiency in raising of hemp and flax; and a town called Weathersfield, on the river, is remarkable for the production of onions, with which it annually loads several vessels to the neighboring provinces.

The trade of this colony to foreign parts is very inconsiderable, they being chiefly supplied with foreign commodities from Boston and New York; in exchange for which they send beef, pork, flax-feed, onions &c.

There are some iron works in this colony carried on to great advantage; and they ship some lumber and horses to the West Indies, and considerable quantities of sassafras to Holland, &c. But, after all, the observation of a nobleman (who from years since, traveled through this and the adjacent provinces) is very just, namely that the "colony of Connecticut may be compared to a cask of good liquor, tapped at both ends, at one of which Boston draws, and New York at the other, till little is left in it but lees and settlings".

They have always been exceedingly careful in this colony not to abuse or exceed the rights and privileges granted them by their charter, whereby they might incur a forfeiture of it; but, in conformity to it continue annually to choose their own Governor, Lieutenant Governor, Assistants and Deputies, &c. by whom all executives officers are appointed and authorized. They generally allow their Governor a very handsome maintenance, and have good funds for other public exigencies.

The religious persuasions here are the same as in the other New England governments; but there are more of the Episcopal Church here than in all the others; nor are they behind hand with the Massachusetts in their care and pains in the educating of their children; the several towns being provided with schools, and those supplied with able masters.

the COLONY of
RHODE ISLAND

THIS colony comprehends what were originally the colonies or plantations of Rhode Island and Providence, being incorporated into one, by a new charter, about the same time as the colony of Connecticut; and like that, they still retain the rights and privileges that were at first granted them in their separate state, keeping up likewise two seats of government, viz. Newport and Providence, at which places their general court is held alternately.

This colony has but a small territory, lying nearly in the figure of a heart, and is bounded north and east by Massachusetts Bay, southerly by the ocean, and westerly by Connecticut.

The principal towns in it are those already mentioned of Newport, situated on the Island called Rhode Island, pleasantly enough, and has a safe and good harbour for ordinary shipping; and Providence, situated not less pleasantly upon Providence River, is a very thriving town, and has a considerable trade.

The number of inhabitants in this colony is computed to be about 70,000.

The soil is generally low, and inclined to rocks and stones; however, when properly improved, produces Indian corn, rye, oats, peas, hemp, flax, and some wheat, and most kinds of fruit common to the climate, in great perfection, especially on Rhode Island itself, which for beauty and fertility, is the garden of the colony, and is exceeded perhaps by no spot in New England. They raise cattle, sheep, and horses in abundance, and the latter the best on the continent. They likewise make considerable quantities of butter and cheese in this country.

The principal commodities exported from hence, are horses, sheep, cheese, and the produce they procure from the neighboring provinces, such as fish and lumber from the Massachusetts and New Hampshire; flour, beef and pork from Philadelphia, New York, and Connecticut, which they commonly pay for in rum, sugar, and molasses, imported from the West Indies, in tea from Holland, or in slaves from the coast of Africa.

The form of government here is in all respects the same as in the colony of Connecticut. They are not, however, so scrupulous in keeping up the terms of their charter, often dispensing with it in some pretty essential points, and taking liberties not only detrimental to the other provinces, but even to the nation, especially in times of war, by carrying on an illicit trade with the enemy, and supplying them with the most material articles. This they have repeatedly done with impunity, to my certain knowledge, in the course of the late war, when many scores of vessels went loaded with beef, pork, flour, &c. under the pretext of flags, which, for a certain confederation, could at any time be procured from their Governor, when at the same time perhaps they carried not more than one or two French prisoners, dividing the crew of one French merchantman they had taken among a whole fleet of flags of truce, laden with articles more welcome to the enemy than all the prisoners, with the ship and cargo, they took from them. Nor can it be greatly wondered at that their Governor should fall in with so clandestine a method for the procurement of a livelihood, when it is considered that they allow him but fifty or sixty dollars per annum for his maintenance; besides, as he is annually elected, so there are always two or more that are competitors for the government; and generally he that distributes the most cash, and gives the best entertainments, let him be merchant, farmer, tradesmen, or what he will, is the man who obtains a majority of votes, which fixes him in the chair (death only excepted) for that year. These election expenses generally run high, as each candidate endeavors to excel his competitor (and, if all put together, would amount to a reasonable maintenance) and must be refunded some way or other during his reign who happens to be elected, and provision made to act the same part over again the next year.

There is in this colony, men of almost every religious persuasion in the world. The greatest number of Quakers, and many have no religion at all, or at least profess none; on which account no questions are asked, every man being left pretty much to think and act for himself, of which neither the laws nor his neighbors take much cognizance, so greatly is their liberty degenerated into licentiousness. This province is infected with a rascally set of Jews, who fail not to take advantage of the great liberty here given to men of all professions and religions, and are a pest not only to this, but the neighboring provinces. There is not one free school in the whole colony, and the education of children, generally, shamefully neglected

the PROVINCE of NEW YORK

THIS province is situated between 40 and 44 degrees north latitude, and 70 and 76 deg. West longitude, being bounded east by the New England provinces, north by the province of Québec, northwest and west by lands of the Five Nations and part of Pennsylvania, southwesterly and southerly by the province of Jersey and the Atlantic Ocean, having a very extensive and valuable territory.

This province (as well as the Jersies and Pennsylvania) was originally settled by the Swedes, not after the New England people settled at Plymouth; and after them some Dutch adventurers settled here, who, being reinforced from Holland, quickly became the strongest party, and obliged the Swedes to acknowledge them as sole proprietors of this country, paying no regard to the claim of the English, who had not only discovered, but traded to it before.

The Dutch founded their claim on a pretence of having purchased it of one Captain Hudson, who had formerly traded on these coasts, and gave name to the river called Hudson's River, and to the bay of the same name to the northward. Under this right, the West India Company sent a number of people to settle here, but were soon after dispossessed by Captain Argal, sent by the province of Virginia, with a proper force for that purpose.

Upon this the above mentioned Company begged permission of King James the first, for some of their people to settle at this place, pretending that it was convenient for their ships to call at for refreshment in their passage to and from the Brazils.

Their request was granted, but upon this express condition that the people who settled there should acknowledge themselves to be under the subject of the King of England. This they accordingly did for some years; but, taking advantage of the troubles that followed in the reign of King Charles the First, the States of Holland shook off their dependence on the crown of England. And gave the before mentioned Company a formal grant of this country; and under this grant they appointed Governors, and erected forts, calling the country Nova Belga, or the New Netherlands; and they also utterly refused to pay to King Charles the Second the sum they had paid to his father and grandfather, for permission to fish on the coasts of Great Britain. These intrusions and usurpations did not occasion an immediate rupture between the two states, as might have been expected; however, not long after, the King made a grant of what is now the province of New York, New Jersey, and Pennsylvania, to his brother James the Duke of York, and High Admiral, who, in the year 1664 sent out a fleet, under the command of Sir Robert Carr, with a sufficient number of land forces, to take passion of the country that had been granted him; who, coming upon the coasts, quickly reduced the forts the Dutch had erected there, and obliged them to become British subjects, or leave the country. The people gladly accepted of the former; whence it was that many of the best families in New York to this day, appear by their names to be Dutch extraction.

New Amsterdam, situated on an island at the mouth of the Hudson's River. Was pitched up for the metropolis, its name being changed to that of New York, in honour of the proprietor's title; and from the name of the city, the country to the east and north, and indeed the whole province, goes under the same appellation; as does likewise the county of Albany, where Dutch had erected a fort, named Orange Fort, receive the name Albany, from the Dukes other title.

The country being thus subdued, Sir Robert returned, taking with him the greatest part of the land forces, and left

the PROVINCE of NEW YORK 49

Colonel Nichols Governor of the country; and as the States General seemed to give up all claim and pretences thereto, it encouraged many people to remove thither from England, so that it soon, by the prudent management of Colonel Nichols making it one of his first studies to cultivate a friendship, and enter into a treaty of peace, with the Mohawks, or Five Nations of the Indians, who have ever since continued true and faithful, and been of great service to this province.

In 1673, a war breaking out between England and the States General, the Dutch sent a fleet to recover this colony, and again reduced it to their obedience; but they kept possession thereof but a very short time, it being ceded to the crown of Great Britain (and the Governor replaced) by the treaty which followed in 1674; ever since which time it hath been under the English government, the people proving peaceable and obedient subjects, ready upon every occasion to extract themselves in defense of the rights of Great Britain, aboard as well as in their own territory; particularly in opposing and repelling the encroachments of the French from Canada, with whom they have had various encounters, being always joined and assisted by the Mohawks, with three hundred of whom, and as many English, Colonel Schyler obtained a complete victory, in the reign of William and Mary, over 700 French regulars, and an equal number of Huron Indians, commanded by the Governor of Québec, near the river St. Lawrence, at which time he would in all probability have routed the French out of Canada, had he had vessels to have crossed the river, and proper artillery. The same Colonel Schyler gallantly repulsed them again in 1716, and destroyed a fort they had erected near Onondaga Lake, with a view to cut off their communication with the Lake Ontario, which is by the way of Albany to Schenectady about twenty miles by land, then up the Mohawk River to Lake Oneida, and from thence to Lake Ontario, without any land carriage, except about a mile at the long falls of the Mohawk River, four miles from that river to the Wood Creek that falls into the Lake Oneida, and about twenty yards to Schuna Falls, near the mouth of Onondaga River, which runs from that lake into Lake Ontario. Soon after this our fort at Oswego was erected, where hath since been carried on the greatest Indian trade of any in America, commanding that of the northern and western Indians; and the French, to make up their loss, while we were supine and careless, erected forts on the river Chamblee or Soriel, at Crown Point, at Niagara, &c. which have since been the source of infinite mischief to this and the New England provinces, till happily reduced and the French excluded from this part of America by the late war.

The City of New York, which is governed by a Mayor and Alderman, is situated on an island bounded by Hudson's River on the west, the Bay and Sound on the south and east, and a small creek or channel communicating with the Sound and Hudson's River, about sixteen miles north from the city. In the city are between 2 and 3,000 houses, generally pretty well built; but the streets very irregular. It hath several spacious public buildings, among which the college and the court house are the most considerable, and the Governor's mansion house within the fort; the houses for public worship are no ways despicable, especially the two English churches. The public worship in this city is every Sunday performed in different churches, in the English, the French, the German, and Low Dutch languages.

This city abounds with many wealthy merchants, who carry on a large trade to foreign parts, and are observed to deal very much upon honour; excepting some Jews, who have been tolerated to settle here, having a synagogue in the city, who sustain no very good character, being many of them selfish and knavish, (and where they have an opportunity) an oppressive and cruel people. The next considerable place in this province is the city of Albany, situated upon the west side of Hudson's River, 150 miles above New York, containing near 400 houses; others are Schenectady, on the Mohawk River, fifteen miles above Albany; Esopus, halfway between Albany and York; and

the PROVINCE of NEW YORK 51

Peckeepsy, about ten miles further down the river. The number of inhabitants in the whole province are about 150,000.

This soil of this province is generally very pleasant and fertile, producing in great abundance all sorts of grain and fruit, common to the climate; especially the intervals, which are many, and large, upon its extended rivers, of which Hudson's River is the chief. This river heads within twenty or thirty miles of Lake Champlain, and runs south for about fifty or sixty miles, crossing in its way some small lakes, of which Scanderoon is the most considerable; it then bends more easterly to the carrying place, where Fort Edward stands; and then southward, till it empties itself into the sea at New York, or Sandy Hook, having on it some exceeding fine intervals at Saratoga, Still Water, Half Moon, the Flats, &c. and below Albany are some islands in it of most excellent land. This river is navigable for vessels of an hundred tons as high as Albany, and schallops can go eight miles above Albany the Mohawk River empties itself at several mouths, called the Sprouts, into this. This river takes its rise in the Mohawk country, and is navigable (excepting some few falls) for whale boats and battoes, for upwards of one hundred miles; its course is eastwardly, and has adjacent to it many fine intervals, particularly that called the German Flats, being settled with Germans, and is extended along the river for fifty miles in length, and about two in width. This track of land is exceeding by none in America, being easy to cultivate, and producing, in the greatest abundance, wheat, barley, peas, hemp, or whatever is put into it. About two miles from where this joins with Hunson's River is a fall or cataract, at which the whole stream descends perpendicular for about seventy feet. This part of the province abounds with saw mills, having great plenty of timber, especially pines.

In the before mentioned rivers is great plenty of fish, such as shad, ail-wives, sturgeon, &c. and also a variety of fresh water fish. In this part of the province are also several iron works, carried on to great advantage; particularly Mr. Levingston's, at his manor, upon Hudson's River, which is said to manufacture the best iron of any in America. There are also very fine lands upon the East River, or Sound, tho' very rocky, as indeed is most of the upland within this province, upon the main land; being mountainous and hard to subdue, yet, when once brought to, it richly rewards the labor of the husbandman. There are also several pleasant and fruitful islands to the south and southeast of the city; and, among these, that called Long Island deserves the first notice. In the sea adjacent to this island are sea bass and black fish in great plenty, which are very good when fresh.

This island is about 150 miles in length, and in some places twenty miles wide; the middle of the island is somewhat barren but both ends are most excellent soil, improved perhaps to as great advantage as any lands in America, producing all kinds of grain and fruit, to be found in this part of the country, to great perfection; and abound with black cattle, sheep, swine, horses, &c. beyond any other part of the province. I am told that the produce of some single acres at the west end, which is handy to New York market annually amounts to near a hundred pounds sterling. And so productive is this island of human species, that no less than a hundred families annually remove from hence to other places, generally carrying with them a handsome sum to begin with; and a much greater number of women are annually married from hence into the neighboring plantations.

There are several other islands belonging to the province, not inferior to this in pleasantness and fertility of soil, tho' of much less extent; as Streighten Island, opposite to the west end of Long Island, forming the Narrows or Straights, thro' which is the passage for ships bound to or from the sea to New York; and Fisher's Island, lying in the Sound, between Long Island and the colony of Connecticut, on the main; and several others, both in the Bay and Sound; one of which in the latter, called Barn Island, about 25 miles from New

the PROVINCE of NEW YORK 53

York, has obtained a charter for erecting a city, and some advances are made towards it.

The situation of New York is extremely happy for trade, having a safe and convenient harbour, accessible three different ways for ships of common burthen, viz. by way of the Sound, between Long Island and Staten Island (which is the most usual and easy entrance); and again between Staten Island and Jersey Shore. There are easy conveyances to and from it by water, upon its rivers and lakes (except some few carrying places) to Montreal and Québec northward, and to the great lakes Erie, Ontario, &c. westward, for 600 miles; and upon the sea it has not only the advantage of its own coasts, but also of Connecticut and the Jersies, their trade in great measure centering here, where they exchange their several commodities for foreign goods.

The commodities exported from hence are therefore those of the three governments, such as wheat, flour, beef, pork, furs and castor, in great abundance; staves, plank, lumber, flax-feed, pig and bar iron, and some copper. And of late great encouragement is given to several manufactories, especially that of hemp, the raising of which is encouraged by a large bounty given by the province; and in the city a society is formed, who sit at stated times, to conduct methods for promoting trade and husbandry in their various branches, and the manufacturing of linen, wool, iron, &c. and considerable premiums are allotted to such as excel in these branches of business; which conduct will doubtless have a tendency to preserve the credit of this province, to enrich the inhabitants, by increasing their exports, and render them less dependant on foreign countries for their commodities and manufactures of several kinds.

His Britannic Majesty is absolute Sovereigness of the soil of this province, and by him the Governor, Lieutenant Governor, Secretary, Council, &c. are appointed; the freeholders of the several counties electing their won representatives, to form a legislative body with them. The cities of New York and Albany have likewise the privilege, by their charters, of making by-laws for themselves, (provided they are not inconsistent with the laws of the province, nor of the realm) which are enacted by the Mayor, Alderman, and Common Council of the respective cities, annually elected by the freemen of each; these likewise form a court of judicature, called the Mayor's court.

The Religious persuasions here are very numerous; there being Episcopalians, Lutherans, Presbyterians, Anabaptist, Moravians, Quakers, and Jews, who not only worship in all their various forms, but as hath been mentioned, in different languages. Learning of late hath been much encountered in the province, the collage being well established, and furnished with a president, professors, and tutors, and a good library; several young gentlemen are annually graduated at it, and the city and county in general are well furnished with schools.

the PROVINCE of
NEW JERSEY

THIS province is situated between New York and Pennsylvania, in a triangular form, having the province of New York northerly, Pennsylvania westerly and southerly, and the Atlantic Ocean easterly, from the mouth of Hudson's River. This province, like New York, was originally settled by the Swedes, and was deemed a part of what the Dutch had possessed themselves of, by the name of Nova Belgia, and was contained in the grant made by King Charles to his brother James, Duke of York, in 1663, who the year following made a grant of that part called New Jersey to Lord Berkley and Sir George Carteret. These two proprietors sent Philip Carteret, Esq. as Governor; and the lands being granted to the settlers for six or seven years, free of quitrents, induced many, especially Dissenters, to come from England, and settle in this country; so that the inhabitants, being a composition of Swedes, Dutch, and English, among whom were some of almost every religious persuasion under heaven; they were like so many jarring elements pent up together, and could not be reduced and reconciled to any settled form of government, but by a military force; they indeed continued within some bounds while they were excused paying quitrents; but after mentioned, when that indulgence was no longer allowed them, and the quitrents afterwards being considerably in arrear, upon the proprietors insisting on payment thereof, they broke out into open rebellion, deposed the Governor, and set up a sort of government of their own, under which they continued till 1673, when they were attacked and subdued by the Dutch; but the country being again restored to the English by the treaty made the following year, Mr. Carteret returned to his government, and the proprietors making some concessions, the inhabitants continued pretty quiet for some time. Lord Berkley soon assigned over the right to Mr. William Penn and three other assignees, with whom Sir George Carteret agreed to divide the country into two equal parts, by running a line from the southeast point of Little Harbour, almost due north; the easternmost part whereof, which on such partition was allotted to Sir George, was and still is called East New Jersey; and the other part which was allotted to Mr. Penn and the other proprietors, was then named West New Jersey, and so became for some time two separate and distinct governments.

Sir George afterwards died and his trustees thereupon sold his right therein to Mr. Penn, and eleven other purchasers; and they not long after sold a part of theirs to the Earl of Perth, and eleven others; all which divisions and subdivisions causing the land to be branched out into such numerous portions, that the respective owners thereof, taking little or no notice of their interests therein, no proper care being taken to settle and fix proper lines and boundaries to their estates, it became difficult, if not impossible, to ascertain their respective rights; which causing from time to time great uncertainty of property, it occasioned so many mobs and tumultuous risings, that the proprietors, being quite wearied out, they in the year 1702 surrendered the entire government of both Jerseys to the crown, reserving only to themselves all their other rights and privileges; and stipulating also for some privileges in favor of the people, which were to be given in charge to all

the PROVINCE of NEW JERSEY 57

future Governors appointed him the crown, as part of their instructions. Upon his surrender, the government of the two Jerseys was by the crown annexed to the government of New York, in which state they continued till the year 1736, when the two Jerseys became one government, and Lewis Morris Esq. was appointed their first Governor, but they still retain a seat of government in each division, at which their assembly and supreme court of justicature sit alternately, viz. at Burlington in West Jersey, and Perth Amboy in East Jersey; which two places, through no ways considerable either for their numbers or trade, have city privileges; as hath the city of New Brunswick, situated upon the River Rariton, about eight miles above Anthony (which stands at the mouth of the river), and is said to be the most flourishing place in the whole province. The number of inhabitants in this province is computed to be about 100,000.

The soil of this province is very uniform, good and easy, natural to wheat and all kinds of English grain, abounding in all kinds of fruit common to the climate; and is said to produce the best cider of any on the continent. The timber is tall, and their oak is in good esteem for ship building. This province abounds in streams of water, convenient for mills, furnaces, or any kind of water works and having great quantities of iron ore, there are in it several furnaces and iron works, and one slitting mill, which are carried on to good advantage. It is likewise supposed to be rich in copper and silver ore, some of both kinds having been found in several parts of the province; but none hath been worked to any great advantage, excepting Schyler's copper mine in East Jersey, about twenty miles west from the city of New York, the produce of which hath already made several fine estates.

There are no rivers of any note that extend far onto this province; that called Passaic, which empties itself into the sea at the northerly part of it, has about twenty miles from its mouth a remarkable fall or cateract, where the whole stream falls seventy feet from a rock whose face is perpendicular.

The lands in this province are chiefly taken up and improved, so that they have but little wild game of any kind; but what greatly obstructs the growth of this province, and hinders it from thriving in proportion to the goodness and fertility of its soil, and making those improvements it is otherwise capable of, is the great uncertainty of their titles, and the continual disputes and law suits which thence arise among the inhabitants, no men growing rich here so fast as the gentlemen of the law. Besides, this province suffers the same fate from Philadelphia and New York, that the colony of Connecticut does from New York, and Boston; having no considerable foreign trade of their own, they exchange their commodities at these two places for foreign goods, and consequently leave a profit there, which otherwise they might have themselves.

The Chief exports of this province are wheat, flour, timber, pig and bar iron, copper ore, and black cattle, which they drive in great numbers to Philadelphia, on whose rich pastures they are generally grazed for some time, before they are killed for market.

The form of government here is the same as that of New York, and the religious persuasions are no less numerous, and much the same as in that province. Here is likewise a collage founded at Prince-Town, about thirty miles from the city of Philadelphia, which is said to be extremely well furnished and regulated, and is much resorted to, not only by the young gentleman of this, but by many of the neighboring provinces.

the PROVINCE of
PENNSYLVANIA

THIS province was by Dutch esteemed a part of their Nova Belgia, and was as such supposed to be included in the grant made by King Charles the Second to his brother James the Duke of York, in 1663, though it does not appear to have been particularly described in the grant. It is situated between 39 and 42 degrees west longitude, being bounded northeasterly by the Jerseys, north by lands of the Five Nations, west by the Appalachian Mountains, and southerly by Maryland. In 1681, Mr. Penn obtained a patent from King Charles for the Upper or inland part of this province; and afterwards, from the Duke of York, he obtained a grant of the sea coasts from the town of Delaware, now Newcastle, to Cape Henlopen. In the country, contained within this last grant, were many Swedes, Dutch, and English settled, who chose to remain under a distinct jurisdiction of their own, but are under the same Governor, and belong to the same proprietor. One of the fundamental regulations of this province, is: " That none who believe in God Almighty, and live peaceably, shall be molested on account of their religious persuasion any religious worship contrary to their declared sentiments" and " That all persons who profess to believe in Jesus Christ, shall not be incapable of serving the government in any capacity on account of any particularities in their religious opinion, they solemnly promising, when required, allegiance to the Proprietor and Governor of the province."

Soon after Mr. Penn had obtained his grant, he engaged and embarked with a considerable number of people to settle in this country, most of whom were Quakers, Mr. Penn himself being of that persuasion; but so upright was he in his proceedings, that although he had, by charter from the King a right to a large extent of country, yet he would not pretend to take possession, or make any division of the lands among his followers, till he had fairly purchased the country of native Indians, in whom he judged the original property and oldest right was vested; and at the same time he engaged the several nations of Indians, inhabiting or claiming this territory, to promise that they would not sell or dispose of any of their lands, but to him, or such as should be authorized by him to purchase the same, giving orders to his agents not to take possession, or suffer any person to take possession of any lands, till they had first made a fair purchase of them from the Indians. This generous procedure of his not only recommended him strongly to the natives, who conceived a very high opinion of his honor and integrity, but laid a foundation for a lasting peace with them, and effectually prevented many of those tragical calamities which several of the American provinces suffered in their infant state. Mr. Penn continued in the country upwards of two years, in which time he formed such an excellent plan for the government of the province as hath since engaged more foreigners to reside here than in any other part of America.

He likewise laid the foundation of the city of Philadelphia, and formed the plan of it, which, for beauty, not only far excels any other in America, but is, perhaps, exceeded by few in the world. This city is situated between two navigable rivers, Delaware on the north, and the Schulkill on the south, which join each other a few miles below, and is near 100 miles from the bay where the river empties itself. The streets are wide and spacious, with a dry defended walk on each side, and are exactly straight and parallel to each other; the houses in general are well built, and make a good appearance, especially some of the public buildings, which are not excelled by any in the country; such, in particular, is the academy, the state house, and several of the churches. The proprietor's seat, which is the

the PROVINCE of PENNSYLVANIA 63

usual place of the governor's residence, and is about a mile above the town, exceeds any private building in America, both in its magnificence and the pleasantness of its situation. This city has exceeding beautiful barracks for the reception of the King's troops, and has the finest market of any on the continent, being of a prodigious extent and well built, and as well regulated and supplied; in short, scarce anything can afford a more beautiful landscape than this city and the adjacent country, which for some miles may be compared to a well regulated flourishing garden, being improved, as I have been informed, to as great advantage as almost any lands in Europe; there are in the city about four thousand inhabitants.

Other considerable places in this province are, first, Lancaster, about sixty or seventy miles from Philadelphia, on the road to Fort Du Quésne or Pittsburg, which is near as large as the city of New York; and about the same distance from Lancaster, on the same road is Carlisle, and about twenty or twenty five miles beyond it, is Shippensburg; the country between Philadelphia and Pittsburg, which are three hundred miles asunder, being pretty well settled for two hundred miles from the former, the land being uniformly good. The number of inhabitants in the whole province of Pennsylvania are upwards of three hundred and fifty thousand.

The most remarkable rivers in this province are the Delaware and the Susquehanna; the first of these takes its rise in the country of the Mohawks or Five Nations, and flows into the sea at Delaware Bay or Cape Henlopen. This river is navigable for near 150 miles up, after which it hath some falls in it, the settlements upon this river extend 150 miles from the city of Philadelphia. The lands adjacent to it are excellent, and scarce ever fail to reward the husbandman in a plentiful manner. This river also affords great plenty and variety of such fish as are common to the climate, especially sturgeon, which are here taken and manufactured in greater abundance than in any other part of America. The general course of the river is nearly southeast.

The Susquehanna takes its rise in the same country, at about 90 miles distance from the Appalachian Mountains, and runs nearly parallel to it, till it empties itself into Chesapeake Bay in Maryland. This river is also navigable in the interior country a great way up, and, if possible, exceeds the other in pleasantness and fertility of the soil adjacent to it, producing in great abundance all sorts of grain common to the climate, especially wheat. But not only the river or intervale lands are exceedingly fruitful and easy to cultivate, producing grain and fruit, hemp and flax, black cattle, sheep, &c. The lands, where improved, are generally well improved, being allotted out to the farmers in such proportions as they are able to manage to advantage, for which they pay an annual quitrent to the lord proprietor. This province likewise abounds in streams fit for any kinds of water works, and manufactures the greatest quantity of iron of any province on the continent. Its forests are as well stored with wild game, as its pastures with flocks and herds; in short, no province on the continent is less dependant on its neighbors, or foreign countries, for either the necessaries or conveniencies and agreeables of life, than this. Its trade is extensive, large, and valuable; no less than three hundred sail annually clearing out from Philadelphia to Europe, the West Indies, &c. Their trade into the interior country, with the Indians is likewise very extensive and lucrative. The chief articles exported from this province, are wheat, flour, bear, pig and bar iron, hogshead and pipe-staves, hoops, furs, peltry, beef, pork, flax-seed, &c.

This is a proprietary government, so styled from the proprietor's being invested with a sort of sovereign authority; he appoints the Governor, Council, and Magistrates; and the representatives of the people are summoned in his name, and by their advice, he enacts laws which are binding, without the approbation of King or parliament at home. But by a late statute, the proprietor

the PROVINCE of PENNSYLVANIA 65

must have the King's approbation in appointing a Governor, when he does not personally reside in the province himself, and of a deputy Governor, when he does. And by another statute, all the Governors in America are liable to be called to an account for mal-administration before the court of King's Bench in England. This province can boast of as great a variety of religious persuasions as that of New York, and perhaps greater here, being, among others, a Popish chapel allowed of; but by far the greatest number are Quakers.

the PROVINCE of MARYLAND

THIS province is next to the southward, being Bounded on the north by Pennsylvania and Delaware Bay; on the east, by the Atlantic Ocean: by Virginia, south; and by the Appalachian Mountains, west; and is divided into the eastern and western divisions by the great bay of Chesapeake.

This province was originally included in the grant made by King James the First to the Southern Company, formed by charter, in 1606; but that grant being vacated, and falling to the crown, this territory was granted by King Charles the First to Lord Baltimore, a Roman Catholic Nobleman, who sent out a number of people to begin the settlement of the country, among whom were several of the Romish persuasion, having obtained an indulgence of enjoying the free exercise of their religion in that country. His Lordships brother embarked in November 1633, and took possession of this country, in honor to Queen Mary, consort to King Charles, was called Maryland. They arrived at the mouth of the Potomac River the March following, and having fixed on a proper place for beginning a settlement, purchased the land of the natives. The place they made choice of was near a small bay at the mouth of the Potomac River, and was a town belonging to the Yoamaco Indians, who having been defeated by the Susquehanna Indians, were come to a resolution to leave their town, and retire further into the country; the English arriving at this happy junction upon fulfilling their agreement, were immediately put in possession of one half of the town. Having thus, by purchase, become masters of a spot of cleared ground, they not only set themselves to building a town called St. Mary's, but to planting of corn; they also purchased what corn they could of the Indians, so that they very soon had a plentiful supply. And as they prudently took care to cultivate a friendship and good correspondence with the Indians, they thereby avoided the distresses which the neighboring colony of Virginia had so often been reduced to, for to this day they have never had any disputes or war with the natives; and in their infant state they were greatly assisted by them, receiving from them plentiful supplies of venison, turkeys, and other gains. But not neglecting the proper means for their security, in case any dispute or misunderstanding should happen, they soon erected a fort, mounting several pieces of cannon, which commanded the town; which so terrified the Indians, that, however they might be disposed, they always behaved peaceably. Being thus happy in the enjoyment of peace and plenty, they soon received reinforcements from England, many of whom were Roman Catholics, on whose account Lord Baltimore, when the legislature was established, procured an act to be passed, which tolerated all who professed Christianity, of whatever persuasion they were.

This colony soon became so considerable, that, at the death of Charles the First, the parliament thought it expedient to take the government of it from the proprietor; nor did Lord Baltimore recover it again till some time after the restoration, when he sent over his son, who continued in the government twenty years, under whose prudent administration the colony flourished exceedingly. Upon his father's death he returned, but first appointed a Gentleman to be Governor in his absence, who held the government till the year 1692, at which time Lord Baltimore was again divested of it, and the right of government assigned to the crown of Great Britain; and, at present, the property of but a small part of the province is vested in Lord Baltimore, he having conveyed by far the greatest part to others.

There are no very considerable towns in this province; the reason of which is, that the plantations being almost al

the PROVINCE of MARYLAND 69

situated upon some navigable creek or river, with which the province abounds, the planters have the convenience of shipping their own produce to England and other parts, and of being supplied from thence with foreign commodities, without having recourse to their merchants.

The principle rivers in this province are Potomac, Patuxent, Pokomoata, Chaptank, and Sassafras River, with many others of smaller note, by which the province is cut and carved into various shapes, and has all the advantages of navigation and water carriage that can be desired. Places of most note in this province are Annapolis, esteemed the capital, St. Mary's, Port Royal, &c.

The number of inhabitants in the province of Maryland is about 85,000 whites, and 25,000 Negroes or slaves.

The air, soil, produce, and commerce of this province being much the same as those of Virginia, I shall describe them conjointly, after first given some account of the rise, &c. of the latter.

Virginia

THIS territory was discovered by Sebastian Cabot, and was the first settled of any in America; for Sir Walter Raleigh, in the year 1584, obtained a grant from Queen Elizabeth, of all remote barbarous and heathen lands he should discover and settle; when he, with Sir Richard Grenville, and several other Gentlemen, at their own expense, fitted out two ships, under the command of Captain Philip Amedas, and Captain Arthur Barlow, who, departing from London in April 1584, on the July following fell in with that part of America now called North Carolina, and landed upon an island which they found covered with cedars, pines, &c. and abounding with deer and other game. This island was called Ocacock, lying at the mouth of New River; at this place, and in the neighboring islands, they were received and entertained by the natives in a friendly manner, with whom they traded, and upon their return to Europe carried two of them to England. They at this time made no settlement in the country, but gave it the name of Virginia, in honor of the virgin Queen. Sir Richard Grenville himself embarked for Virginia the spring following, having seven ships under his direction carrying with him, as an interpreter, one of those Indians that had been brought to England the preceding year, and arrived at the island Ocacock the 26th of May. From hence they passed over to the continent; but a dispute arising between an Indian and one of Sir Richard's followers, they imprudently burnt the Indian town, destroyed their corn, and did them other considerable damages; which gave the Indians very unfavorable ideas of these newcomers, and was, it may be supposed, the cause of their behaving in a quite different manner from what they had done formerly. Sir Richard, returning to England, left on the island Roanoke upwards of a hundred men, to make a settlement there, under the care of one Mr. Lane; but they met so many interruptions from the Indians, were so frequently in danger of being cut off by them, and in time reduced to such distress, that they were glad to return to England with Sir Francis Drake, who called there in his return from an expedition against the Spaniards.

Sir Walter Raleigh had, before these people arrived in England, sent out a ship with provisions and other necessaries, for the supply of the infant colony, Sir Richard Grenville following soon after with three ships more; but this first ship, not finding any of the people, returned to England; and upon Sir Richard's arrival he neither found the ship nor the people he had left there the year before. This greatly discouraged him; however, not to give up the undertaking, he left fifty men at the fort on Roanoke, with a supply of necessaries for two years, and sailed for England. The next spring three ships more were sent out, under the direction of Captain White, with a supply of provision and men, who upon his arrival found nothing but a skeleton of one of the people, and the fort destroyed; what became of the rest was never known.

These repeated misfortunes however did not dismay those adventures; for, in spite of the disasters their countrymen had met with, they determined to erect a fort, and keep possession of the island they were then upon, called Cape Hatteras; and Mr. White, by the choice of the rest, was sent home to solicit a fresh supply; but upon his arrival, an embargo was laid upon all shipping, on account of the expected invasion from the famous Spanish Armando. However, after great importunity, and much difficulty, he obtained permission to sail with two small ships, both of which were intercepted by the Spaniards, plundered and obliged to put back to England. No care after this was taken to send relief to the brave adventurers, till the month of March 1590, when three ships were fitted out at the expense of some merchants, to whom Sir Walter Raleigh had assigned over his right to Virginia; but though they sailed

VIRGINIA 73

from Plymouth in March, they never arrived at Cape Hatteras till the next August, having employed themselves all that time in plundering some Spanish islands. When White arrived he could find no sign of his countrymen, but the word Croatan cut on a wooden post; for it had been agreed when White left that island, that they should leave some such signal, with the name of the place they intended to remove to. It was therefore imagined that they were gone to and island of that name, but now called Cape Lookout. Accordingly, they directed their course for that place; but meeting with bad weather, his people grew uneasy. Being impatient to get home with their plunder, they obliged him to steer for England, without once searching the island Croatan for their unfortunate countrymen; and, it is presumed, they all either perished with hunger, or were destroyed by the savages, as none of them were ever heard from afterwards, though ships were immediately sent out by Sir Walter Raleigh in search of them. All thoughts of settling Virginia which was then a general name for the whole Northern Continent, were now laid aside for some years; but so favorable were the accounts of the country, that the project was received again in 1606, when two companies were formed, consisting not only of merchants, but several Noblemen and Gentlemen joined in the design; one of these companies was for the southern, the other for the northern colony.

Sir Thomas Smith, a rich merchant in London, and one of those to whom Sir Walter Raleigh had assigned over his right, was president of the former company, by whom three ships were fitted out with men, provisions, and every necessary for making a settlement, with proper directions for establishing a form of government. They arrived at Virginia in April, at the mouth of Chesapeake Bay, lying between two capes, to which they gave the names of Cape Henry and Cape Charles, after the King's two sons. Here they searched for some time in quest of a proper place to erect a fort, and begin a settlement; and at last pitched upon a peninsula, about forty miles from the mouth of the River Pacohatan. To this place they gave the name James Town, from whence the river has since obtained the name James River.

The Indians, for several days after they landed, kept them in constant alarms, by frequently attacking them; but not long after they sued for peace, which was the more readily granted them on account of their ships returning to England; which they did a few days after, leaving one hundred men, many of whom were soon after taken sick, owing, as was supposed, to their bad provisions. One Wingfield, who was sent out as their President, behaved in such a manner that they were obliged to deprive him of his presidency, and elect another. But the management of affairs chiefly depended on Captain Smith, who had during the passage been very ill used, and for three months confined by Wingfield; but on their coming on shore, Smith insisted upon being brought to trial, where his innocence appeared so conspicuous, that Wingfield was condemned in two hundred pounds damages; which recovery Mr. Smith generously gave up for the service of the colony. It was owing to the prudence, judgment, and fortitude of this Gentleman, that these adventurers were not, like their predecessors, destroyed. By his example he encouraged his companions to labor; his courage was a terror to the savages, whose treacherous schemes for the destruction of the settlement he seasonably discovered, and wisely prevented their taking effect. It was through his influence and persuasion that his companions did not abandon the settlement and return to Europe, in a bark that had been left them, in order that they might extend their trade with the natives, and make further discoveries up the country. But, notwithstanding such signal services, envy, the constant attendant on true merit, was employed in raising objections to Mr. Smith's conduct; and, having nothing of more importance to find fault with, blamed him for not going in search of the head of Chickahomia River. Though it was

VIRGINIA 75

not the least consequence to the colony, yet he resolved to remove this cavil, by endeavoring to find the source of the river. He embarked in a barge, and going as far as that would carry them, with two Englishmen and two Indians, he took to a canoe, leaving orders with those in the barge, that not any of them should go ashore till he returned; but scarce had he turned his back before his orders were disobeyed, and they surprised by a party of Indians, consisting of 300, headed by a brother of the King of Pamunkey; one George Caffan, was taken prisoner, the rest narrowly escaped; the chieftain, called Opechankanough, extorted from Caffan which way Mr. Smith was gone, and then cruelly put him to death. Captain Smith, having proceeded up the river till it terminated in a swamp, left the canoe in care of two Englishmen, while he himself went to kill some provisions. The two men were surprised asleep, and killed by the before mentioned party, who tracked the Captain and surrounded him; he however made a brave defense, killed three of the Indians and wounded several others, so that none cared to approach him; he received a slight wound in his thigh, and had several sticking in his clothes; but, attempting to gain his canoe, he suddenly fell into a bog up to his middle. Being benumbed and almost dead with cold, they drew him out, carried him to the fire, where his men had been killed, and rubbed and chaffed his benumbed limbs.

Upon Mr. Smith's recovering his senses, he was brought before Opechankanough, to whom he presented an ivory compass. The savage was very much surprised at the motion of the needle, which he could see through the glass, but could not touch, and was much astonished on having the use of it explained to him; yet soon after the Indians tied Mr. Smith to a tree, and were preparing to shoot him, but were prevented by their chief holding up the compass. They then carried him off in great triumph to a hunting town, much resorted to by King Pawhaten and his family, called Orapakes, carrying the English swords and muskets, the trophies of their victory, before them, and Captain Smith under a guard of six Indians. The women and children flocked out to behold one of their species so very unlike any they had hitherto seen, but treated Mr. Smith with whatever their town afforded; and one of them for a trifling present of beads, returned him his coat, which seasonably defended him against the inclemency of the weather, it being extremely cold. During these transactions, Mr. Smith had a very narrow escape; the father of the Indians he had wounded, in making his defense, rushed upon him; but his guards protected him from this savage. They showed Mr. Smith the preparations they were making to attack James Town, and asked his advice, promising his liberty. If he would lend them his assistance. He dissuaded them from making any such attempt, describing to them the springing of mines, the great guns, &c. in such a manner as both amazed and intimidated them; and persuaded some of them to go to James Town for some toys, he, by means of a table-book, acquainted his companions of the enemies intention, requesting at the same time to be sure to send the several articles he wrote for, and instructed them how they should terrify and affright the messengers.

In three days they returned from James Town, and were not only themselves surprised, but the rest at their relation, to find everything had happened as he had told them, and that the table-book could speak. Having laid aside their intention of attacking James Town, they carried Mr. Smith from Pamunkey or James River round the country to Potomac, and then brought him back again, tho' many different tribes of Indians, to Pamunkey. They then for some days conjured him, by many frightful ceremonies, to know whether he intended them good or ill? He was then invited and seated by Opitchanpan, second brother of Pawhatan; but in no place would any of the Indians eat with him, tho' they eat heartily of his leavings. At length he was conducted to the imperial seat, the residence of Pawhatan, situated on the north side of York River, as it is now called. This Indian Emperor lived in great state and magnificence

VIRGINIA 77

(according to the savage customs of the country) having generally forty or fifty of his tallest subjects to attend upon his person; which guard was now, thro' fear of the English, increased to 200, who by turns kept sentry every night at the four corners of his palace. He had no less than thirty Kings tributary to him, who were all obliged to govern their subjects agreeable to his laws. When Mr. Smith was presented to him, his Imperial Majesty was seated before a fire, clothed with a mantle of raccoon skins, with a plume of feathers on his head, attended by a number both of men and women, ranged on each side, all painted and ornamented after the manner of their country; as he entered the house, they all gave a loud shout; there was then brought him a calabash of water to wash his hands, by the Queen herself, and having entertained and feasted him in their best manner, they entered into a long consultation; at the conclusion of which two large stones were brought and placed before Pawhatan, and Mr. Smith's head laid upon them, in order to have his brains beat out with clubs; which act could only be prevented by Pocahantas, the King's favorite daughter, who, seeing in-treaties would not avail, clasped his head in her arms, and laid her own upon it, to save his life.

Mr. Smith likewise received many instances of friendship from the Emperor's son, who was the most comely and manly person in Pawhatan's court. A few days after this, Pawhatan acquainted Mr. Smith that they were now friends, that he might now return to James Town, that he loved him equal to his son, that he would give to him a part of the country; but that he should send him two great guns and a grind stone. Mr. Smith did not much depend on his friendship; but being immediately sent off with a proper convoy, arrived next day at James Town, having been a captive seven weeks. He entertained the convoy in the most friendly manner, showed them two great guns and a grind stone, to carry to the Emperor; but their weight being superior to their strength, he dismissed them with such presents for their master, and his people, as proved agreeable.

Affairs at James Town, in his absence, had got into great confusion, the people were dispirited, and about to quit the inhospitable shore in the vessel that had been left them; but upon his representing to them the absurdity of such a resolution, the plenty in which he had seen the natives live, and the fertility of the soil, he brought them to a different mind, they resolving to maintain their fort, and provide fro themselves in this resolution a few days after, when Pocahontas came to the fort with a numerous train, bringing a large supply of all kinds of provisions which the country then afforded; which she continued to do every four of five days, for some years afterwards; for Mr. Smith's behavior, while amongst them, had given the Indians a very high opinion of the courage and knowledge of the English, and the most terrible apprehensions of their instruments of war. This doubtless paved the way for Pocahontas to save his life, which her passion for him induced her to do, and afterwards to visit and supply the fort; so that the passion of this savage princess, then about fourteen years of age, seems to have, in some sort, laid a foundation for the first Christian settlement in America, or at least contributed much to the establishment of it.

In 1607 the colony received a supply, two ships having been sent out by the company, with 120 men, provisions, &c. which were loaded back with furs, skins, and other produce of the country. Captain Smith had by this time gained a pretty thorough knowledge of the adjacent country, and the several rivers in it; but the company in England, by the insinuations of one Captain Newport, fell upon measures which Captain Smith could not approve of, foreseeing that they would be detrimental to the colony. This made Newport his declared enemy, and during his stay in the country his conduct was such as quite altered the opinion they had conceived of the English; so that, upon Newport's departure, Mr. Smith found it difficult to procure a sufficiency of provisions, and would have been cut off in an excursion he made with a party for this end, had it not been for his faithful friend the Princess Pocahontas, who ventured herself through the darkness of the night to give him intelligence of Indians design. Pawhatan had been supplied privately from the fort at James Town, by some villains that were confederates with him, with some muskets, swords, powder and shot. Notwithstanding Mr. Smith's wise and prudent conduct, which had now more than once saved the colony from entire ruin; yet such complaints by some ill minded persons were carried home against him, as greatly lessened his credit with the company, who being likewise disappointed in their sanguine expectations of golden hills and silver mountains in this country, applied for a new charter; which was easily obtained, and granted to a number of noblemen, gentlemen, and merchants, who still flattered themselves that higher up the country were rich and valuable mines, so many persons of rank and fortune engaged in the design, the sum raised by them enabled the managers to fit out nine ships, with 500 settlers, and all necessaries for them.

They embarked in May 1609. Sir Thomas Gates, Sir George Summers, and Captain Newport, being all in one ship, were separated in a gale of wind from the rest, and shipwrecked among the Bermuda Islands. The rest of the fleet at Virginia. Mr. Smith found it very difficult to procure subjection to his government from those newcomers, as they daily expected he would be superceded in the direction of affairs; he however carried his point, and would have maintained his authority till the new commission arrived, and in all probability have preserved the colony from those distresses it afterwards fell into, had it not been for the misfortune that befell him in his return from the Falls of James River, where he had been to make a new settlement; as he was sleeping in his boat, his powder flask, by some accident took fire, which wounded him to that degree as put him to exquisite pain, and greatly endangered his life; being in this situation unable to quell those factions which daily arose, and not properly provided at this place with a surgeon and medicines, he embarked for England, leaving the colony well supplied with all necessaries, and their neighbors the Indians subdued, and terrified at the very name of an Englishman; so that this Gentleman is justly esteemed the first founder of an English colony in America. But such was the return he met with for all his services, that, no sooner had he brought the enterprise to bear, than he was superseded in his command, and never received the least benefit or reward for all he had done.

The three Gentlemen who suffered shipwreck on the Bermuda Islands found means to get from thence, by building two small barks, and arrived at Virginia in the month of May the year following, where they found matters in greatest confusion, the colony being reduced to famine, and other accidents, to sixty men, women and children, out of near five hundred left there by Mr. Smith about eight months before; for the Indians, apprized of Mr. Smith's departure, did not only refuse to furnish them with any provisions, but murdered the people where and when ever they could; among which unhappy victims was Mr. Radcliff, one of Mr. Smith's greatest enemies, who, confiding in the insidious promises of Pawhatan, was cut off with thirty men.

The above Gentlemen, finding the distressed situation of the colony, determined to leave the unfortunate shore and return to England; and accordingly embarked, leaving the fort standing; but before they could reach the mouth of the river they were met by Lord Delaware, with three ships, from England, loaded with all kinds of stores and necessaries for the use of the colony, and a supply of people, with whom they all returned to James Town, where his Lordship having landed and opened his commission, his rank, joined to his personal endowments, procured him great authority, and restored peace, industry, and frugality among the people; and, by some well timed severities to the Indians, he checked their incursions, and by lenity and acts of kindness won over others, so that the colony was plentifully supplied with corn, but with their hogs and poultry having been entirely destroyed, Sir George Summers sailed for Bermuda, to fetch a fresh supply, but was there taken sick and died; and the crew, instead of returning to Virginia, sailed for England.

Lord Delaware being obliged to return to England for recovery of his health, the government devolved upon Sir Thomas Dale, who now arrived from England with three ships having on board a large reinforcement of men for the colony, a large supply of provisions, and a number of live cattle, which they were more particularly in want of. This Gentleman brought over a body of laws, by virtue of which he divided the lands, obliging every one to plant corn for his own supply. Sir Thomas Yates arrived this year in August, with six ships, 300 men, 100 head of live cattle, 200 hogs, ammunition and necessaries of all kinds; to whom Sir Thomas Dale resigned his commission, as being the superior officer, and proceeded to make a settlement higher up in the country, at the mouth of the Appomatox River; but the supplies from England this year were so scanty, that they were obliged to purchase corn of the Indians.

Captain Argal, who commanded one of the last ships that arrived, was sent to the River Potomac for that purpose; for Pawhatan and the neighboring Indians refused to deal with them. At the court of Japazaws, King of Potomac, was Pocahontas, who for a trifling present was yielded up to Argal. This Princess, through she continued a friend to the English, had never visited James Town after the departure of Captain Smith; it was attempted by means of Pocahontas to bring Pawhatan to terms, but to no purpose; he refused to ransom her, or to deal with them, till Sir Thomas Dale, taking with him 150 men, went to his capital, and threatened to burn it and all that belonged to him. In the mean time Pocahontas had gained the affections of one Mr. Rolfe, a young Gentleman of character in the Colony, and a marriage being agreed upon by all parties, they were married in April 1613, in presence of her uncle and two brothers, whom her father sent to be witnesses, refusing to be present himself, or upon any occasion to put himself in the hands of the English. From this marriage are descended some of the first families in Virginia.

In 1616 Sir Thomas Dale arrived in England, leaving the government to his deputy, Mr. George Yeardly. Argal being appointed Deputy Governor, occasioned some disturbances by his extraordinary proceedings, which induced the Lord Delaware (ever anxious for the good of the colony) once more to offer his service in it; but upon his passage he died at the mouth of Delaware Bay, from whence it derives its name. Sir George Yeardly was then appointed Governor, who called the first assembly, which consisted of the Gentleman of the Council, and two members from each of their boroughs, the country at that time not being divided into counties; from whence the lower house of assembly to this day is called the house of burgesses. Great improvements were made, and many useful regulations set on foot, during the government of Sir George; Lands were laid out and assigned for the support of public use, and the colony was in a most flourishing situation.

Nothing material happened till 1612, when the utter destruction of the whole colony was concerted by the Indians, now commanded by Opechankanough, his brother Pawhatan being dead. The Indians were incensed at this time at the death of one of their chiefs, who was killed by two servants in revenge for his having killed their master; however, this subtle commander and his people so artfully disguised their resentment and cruel intentions, that the English had not the least mistrust of their plot, and would have been wholly unprepared to have prevented the execution of it (which was to have been on the 22nd day of March) had it not been for an Indian who was converted to Christianity, and lived with Mr. Pace. This Indian's brother, coming to sleep with him the night before, informed him of what was intended the next day, which he communicated to Mr. Pace the next morning, who took all possible pains to spread the alarm, that the English might be prepared for their enemies, who were posted in parties over the whole country; but in spite of precautions, the savages killed 350 men, women and children; when finding the settlement alarmed, they retreated with precipitation.

The out plantations upon this were deserted, their corn and cattle destroyed, great difficulties ensued to the colony; but being reinforced from England, they made reprisals on the Indians, plundered their towns, and killed them wherever they found them, burnt their houses, and left many of them to perish in the woods with mere famine; their frightened remains were glad to retire to a great distance, leaving our people masters of their country. But their perfidious leader survived to create new troubles afterwards, when he took advantage of some political disturbances and confusion that happened in the colony, and determined once more to attempt the destruction of it; in which he so far succeeded as to cut off great number of back inhabitants.

About this time the government was taken from the company, and vested in the crown, retaining very near the same form and laws; and Sir John Hervey was appointed the first King's Governor, whose despotic and partial administration gave great uneasiness, and produced repeated complaints against him, which not being listened to, the council and assembly united in seizing him, and sending him prisoner to England, where his accusers could not be admitted to a hearing (their conduct being an act of open rebellion) and he was sent back with as ample authority as ever; but scarce had he embarked before he was recalled, and Sir William Berkley appointed in his room, whose administration being quite the reverse of the other's quickly put a new face on the affairs of the colony, which upon his arrival he found in the utmost confusion and consternation; for the Indians had fallen suddenly on the back settlers, and had killed 500 men, women and children. Sir William soon retaliated upon them; for, having intelligence that Opechankanough with his followers were encamped at the head of James River, he went with a select body of horse, fell suddenly upon them, and obtained a complete victory. Their leader was killed, and the several tribes he commanded now separated, choosing Kings of their own and sued for peace, which was granted them, and the back settlements secured, the people made easy, increased in riches and numbers. So that by his wife and prudent management this province, when the Civil War broke out in England, could raise several thousands of fighting men.

Sir William retained his command till after the decollation of King Charles when the parliament sent out a fleet to reduce Virginia, which the Governor would have opposed, but the Council and assembly declaring against it, he was obliged to submit, after procuring a general indemnification for himself and the colony. He then lived upon his own plantation till a little before the death of Cromwell, when Matthews, Cromwell's Governor, dying, and no provision being made in case of such a contingency, the people applied to Sir William, to take upon him the government. Which he refused, unless, with him, they would venture their lives and fortunes, and declare for the King. Which they agreed to, and Charles the Second was proclaimed, in whose name he acted and issued all his orders. This brave and loyal conduct was highly approved of by the King; upon his restoration, Sir William's commission was renewed, and he was permitted to come to England, after appointing a Deputy Governor, where the King gave him a most favorable reception, and made him one of the patentees of South Carolina.

Sir William returned to his government in 1662, where he soon found some uneasiness and discontent, on account of some acts having passed, limiting the trade of the colonies, from which some of the Protector's soldiers, who had retired here, took encouragement to form a party, and set up an independent government of their own. Their design was

VIRGINIA 85

seasonably discovered and prevented, by hanging some of the ringleaders.

Soon after this another faction broke out, headed by one Bacon, a young Gentleman of fortune in the colony, on pretence of being revenged on the Indians, who had committed some outrages on the frontiers, they made some extraordinary demands, which not being fully gratified, they burnt James Town. Their leader dying, and a general pardon being promised them, they returned to their obedience. Sir William returned to England, to whom succeeded Lord Culpepper, and after him General Spotswood; and so a succession of Governors to the present Sir Jeffrey Amherst, the province commonly being governed by some Nobleman or General Officer.

Nothing very material has happened in the province from that time to the beginning of the late war, in which its frontiers suffered greatly from the French and Indians, even though the Province has not been backward in raising and supporting troops, and in granting all reasonable assistance during the whole war. The remains of the Virginian Indians, after Sir William Berkley, were set upon by the Mohawk or Five Nations, who drove them out of the province. They then dispersed to different points of the compass, and to various Indian nations for protection, so that the very name of them is now lost.

Virginia has a very extensive territory, being situated between 36 and 39 degrees north latitude, and 74 and 80 degrees west longitude; indeed by their charter they have right to the whole country west and northwest to the south sea. It lies upon the Great Bay of Chesapeake, formed by the Promontories called Cape Henry and Cape Charles, and is perhaps as fine an inland bay as any in the world. Running up thro' Virginia and Maryland near due north 130 miles, and is navigable the whole way for large ships, being in most places twenty miles across. This province has also four fine rivers flowing into the west side of the bay, which take their rise in the Appalachian Mountains, running from northwest to southeast. The southernmost of these is James River (called by the Indians Pawhatan) about two miles broad, and navigable at least for fourscore miles. The next is the York River (called by the Indians Pamunkey) which is also navigable a great way up, and in some places comes very near the former. A little further north is the River Rappahannock, navigable a great way, and in some places comes within a few miles of the York River.

The northernmost is the great River Potomac, which is navigable quite to the falls, being accounted 200 miles, and is in many places nine miles over. These four rivers or creeks, which flow into them, being navigable for small craft, render this country the most commodious for water carriage of any in America. Most of the plantations are situated upon or very near these rivers, every planter has the conveniency of shipping his goods for England, or wherever he sends them, and receiving from thence, in return, such necessaries as they stand in need of. Hence it is, that many of the planters live upon their own estates, and have no occasion to apply to merchants in any of the sea ports. This is the reason that there are no considerable towns in this province. The town of most note is Williamsburg, to which the seat of government hath been transferred from James Town, on account of its being both a more commodious and healthy situation. This town is within land, between two navigable creeks running out of York and James Rivers, by which means it hath and easy communication with both; and chiefly consists of one straight street, about a mile long from east to west; at the west end stands the college, and on the right hand of the street that leads to the college stands the Governor's house, built by the province for his residence, an elegant seat, being enclosed with a beautiful walk of trees, and elegantly finished both inside and out; the courthouse likewise, and other public buildings, are very spacious and elegant.

VIRGINIA

As we approach this country from the ocean, the face of it appears low and level, and for a hundred miles within land scarce a hill is to be seen, or a stone to be found; the soil fertile, producing wheat, barley, Indian corn, and tobacco; which last is the staple commodity of this province and Maryland. Above the Falls the country grows hilly, and afterwards mountainous, interspersed with valleys, extremely pleasant as well as fruitful.

The further you travel into the country, the more healthful it is; so that the inland parts of the province will probably hereafter be most populous and pleasant. From these mountains descend the rivers that have been mentioned, and several that floe westward into the Ohio, by which there is an easy communication between the Mississippi and Lake Erie. This whole country was called by the natives Savannas, or the Low Country, it being as hath been observed, for a great way from the sea, one entire plain. The trees grow very lofty; nor is the ground encumbered with underwood, so as to hinder their being traveled thro' on horseback, affording a commodious shade to those who pass thro' them

The heat and cold, both here and in Maryland, are governed by the winds; the north and northwest winds are commonly cold and clear, the south and southeast moist, hazy, and very hot; in winter the air is clear and dry; the fronts do not continue long, but are sometimes very severe, freezing the rivers over, tho' three miles across; the snow falls sometimes in large quantities, but rarely continues long. The months of May and June are very pleasant, July and august are generally excessive hot; and in September and October the rains fall, when the inhabitants, for the most part, become sickly, being subject to agues, intermitting fevers, &c. Altho' the soil of these provinces is generally shallow and sandy, yet no country produces such excellent tobacco; the lands indeed soon wear out, unless improved by digging and manuring. The woods abound with great variety of flowers of sweet scented shrubs; here is the large tulip laurel, the bark of whose roots, in intermitting fevers, has been found to answer all the purposes of the famous Peruvian Bark.

If the planters did not find sufficient emoluments arise from raising tobacco, they might here manufacture most kinds of naval stores, such as pitch, tar, turpentine, masts, yards, planks, &c.

The chief exports from these provinces, besides tobacco, are iron, beef, pork, pipe staves, and other lumber. Besides the animals in common, such as black cattle, horses, sheep, hogs, &c. which are very numerous, they have many peculiar to the country, as there are in the other provinces of America. Poultry here is remarkable cheap, and wild fowl, even during the winter season, are in the greatest plenty. But all other commodities and productions of this country are swallowed up in that of tobacco, the importance of which trade to Great Britain will easily appear from the shipping employed, and the quantity imported from hence, and again exported to foreign markets; it being computed, that generally one year with another, 200 large ships are freighted with that commodity, and that 100,000 hogsheads are yearly exported, each weighing 400 weight, out of which it is supposed that 40,000 hogs heads are consumed at home, and the other 60,000 exported from Great Britain to foreign markets (most of it after being manufactured at home) for which we either receive cash, or such articles as otherwise we should be obliged to pay a modern author, to show how much this commodity alone contributes to preserve the general balance of trade in our favor, and how much it imports us not only to protect the colonies of Virginia and Maryland, but also to prevent as much as possible their laboring men from being drawn away from their labor, in order to defend themselves and their country. But besides the tobacco, we have many other sorts of goods imported from Virginia and Maryland, as every one may see from the bills of entry from thence; and as the soil is in general good, in many parts rich, we may expect that

VIRGINIA 89

imports of all kinds will increase, especially when we consider that it is not yet 150 years since our first colony settled in this country.

"Add to these advantages, the vast number of people that are employed, maintained, and many of them enriched here at home, by the industry of their countrymen in these colonies; for except their daily food, there is scarce anything they make use of, but what is manufactured in, or sent there from the mother country; and the shipping employed in the trade supports a considerable number of our naval force. But the two last advantages we reap from all our colonies in America, &c.

The annual revenue arising to the crown from tobacco only, is very considerable; and several hundred thousand are employed in. and supported by, raising and manufacturing it. There is also a considerable revenue arising to the crown, from a quitrent paid annually by the owners of all passengers who come into the province, from a duty on liquors and slaves, and from fines and forfeitures.

It hath already been observed, that the King of Great Britain has the appointment of the Governor in this province, and in him and his council the supreme jurisdiction of civil affairs is lodged, who sit twice a year for that purpose with the Burgesses or representatives of the people.

There are but three public officers besides the Governor that are commissioned immediately from the King, viz. the Auditor of the Revenue, the Receiver General, and Secretary; in the office of the latter are proved and recorded all deeds, wills, &c. The Public Treasurer is appointed by the assembly, The Governor is, by his commission Lieutenant General of the militia of the province, who appoints in each county a colonel, and Lieutenant Colonel, and all other commissioned officers. All between the ages of sixteen and sixty years (not otherways excused) are obliged to bear arms, and attend a general muster once a year in the country where they dwell, and four times a year in smaller parties, or single companies.

The number of inhabitants in this province is about 200,000 whites, and it is supposed there are half that number of negroes or slaves.

The religion professed in this province by the generality is that of the church of England.

Ecclesiastical affairs are under the inspection of a commissary, authorized by the Bishop of London, who presides over all the colonies in religious matters for the promotion of learning in this province, a college was early founded at Williamsburg, consisting of a President, six Professors, and one hundred students; for endowing which King William not only gave 200 I. but granted 20,000 acres of land, and a penny per pound on all tobacco exported; it hat also received several other valuable donations, and, upon the whole, is one of the richest colleges in America.

VIRGINIA

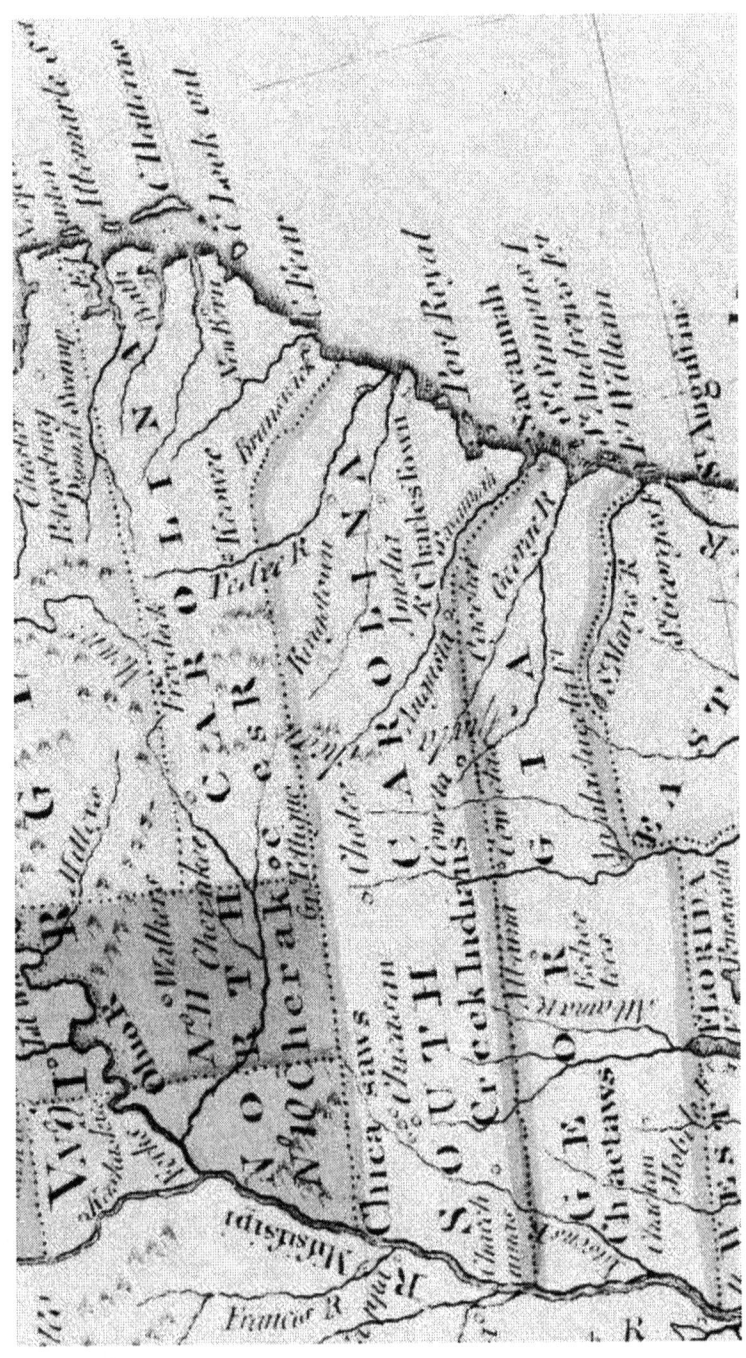

NORTH & SOUTH CAROLINA and GEORGIA

THESE, which are now three distinct governments, were originally but one, extending from 30 to 36 degrees of north latitude, and from 75 to 86 west longitude, being bound on the north by Virginia, east by the Atlantic Ocean, south by St. John's River, and west by Mississippi.

This extensive territory is a part of the discoveries made by the Cabots in 1497; but nothing having been done here in consequence of their discovery, the Spaniards, in 1512, attempted a settlement on that part called Florida; but not succeeding, they abandoned the country, which lay neglected by the Europeans, till 1560, when Coligni, the famous French Admiral, sent out two ships, under the command of one Monsieur Ribaut, to make a settlement on the coast of Florida. Accordingly Ribaut landed in several places to the north of Altamaha River, taking possession of the country in the name of his master, which he called Carolina, in honor of his sovereign Charles IX, and at last settling at the mouth of Albemarle River, erected a fort there, to which he gave the name of Charles Fort. But a civil war breaking out in France soon after, he was under necessity, for want of supplies, to abandon the settlement; and had he not met with an English Ship which furnished him with provisions, he and his people would have, in all probability, perished by famine. Coligni, not disheartened by this, fitted out six ships, under the command of Monsieur Ribaut and on Laudoner, in 1564 and 1565, to reestablish the settlement, of which the Spaniards having received information, they sent out a force to oppose him, and reduce the fort; Ribaut being first killed in defending it, and

Laudoner with the remains of his people returned to France. The Spaniards left a garrison in the fort, as if they intended to keep and enlarge their acquisition, but being attacked by the French, commanded by one De Gorques, they drove out of the country. De Gorques demolishing all the forts they erected, and laid waist their settlements, returned to France, and the Civil War still continuing, no further attempts were made towards a settlement in Carolina, and this fine country lay unnoticed for almost a whole century, that is, till 1663, when our King Charles II resolved to assert his right to it; and to encourage the planting of a colony here, he granted it by patent, bearing date March 24, 1663, including all the territory from the north end of Chikehaul Island, in 36 degrees north latitude, south to the river Matteo, now Altamaha, in 31 degrees north latitude, and so west as far as the South Seas, to eight proprietors, viz. the Duke of Albemrle, the Earl of Clarendon, Lord Craven, Lord Berkeley, Lord Ashley (afterwards created Earl of Shaftsbury), Sir George Carteret (ancestor to the present earl of Granville), Sir William Berkeley, and Sir John Colleton; but there being some errors in the patent, with regard to the boundaries, a new one was made out two years afterwards, by which both the southern and northern boundaries were extended, the former to St. John's River, and the latter to Virginia.

A form of government was drawn up, and 12,000 pounds raised by the proprietors, to defray the charges of tools, &c. for those who were sent over to begin the settlement: but what greatly contributed to the sudden peopling of this colony, were some severities used at home towards dissenters, who on that account, flocked here in great numbers, full toleration being given to people of every profession, so that in 1670 a numerous colony was sent over under Col. William Sayle, who was appointed the first Governor. The year following they were reinforced, and received a good supply of necessaries. The lands were laid out to each man in proportion to the number of his family, subject to a small quitrent, with an obligation to clear and plant a certain quantity of land within a time specified. By this prudent regulation, the colony was soon able to provide itself with most necessaries, and having met with no disturbance from the natives, they were enabled to carry on two settlements at the same time, viz. one at the mouth of Ronoack River to the North, and another southward, at the confluence of Ashley and Cowper. Rivers. This last town was, in honor to the then reigning King called Charles Town, which has since been the metropolis of South Carolina.

The natives gave no interruption to the planters for the first ten years, nor till their avarice and injustice excited them to it, for they set up the shameful trade of purchasing of the Indians such prisoners as they took in their wars with one another, and afterwards sold them as slaves, either to Spaniards, or to our own planters in the West Indies islands, at which the Indians were so exasperated, that they took up the hatchet against them; but however, such was the courage and good conduct of Mr. Joseph West, their Governor at that time, that no very ill consequences followed upon this rupture, the Indians being soon reduced to terms of peace, and the colony rested in quiet, till disturbed by their own domestic jars and animosities, which first arose on account of the quitrents they were obliged to pay to the proprietors, or their assigns, each of whom had a seat in the assembly. The quitrents many of the planters refused to pay; this consequently produced a dispute between the deputies af the proprietors and the representatives of the people. This flamed, however to no great degree, till blown up by a disputed election of a Governor, on the decease of Joseph Blake, Esq.: for it had been the custom, that the proprietors deputies chose a successor to the government, who was by the proprietors either confirmed, or another sent in his room. The Gentleman elected at this time, contrary to the minds of the greater part of the people, was James Moore, Esq.; who found interest to be confirmed, and by several instances rendered himself still more odious to those who opposed him; especially by a fruitless and unsuccessful expedition, which he made, in 1702, against the Spanish Settlement at St. Augustine. The murmurs and complaints that ensued obliged the proprietors to displace him; and in his room they appointed Mr. Nathaniel Johnson, who, in 1704, perfectly completed the disaffection of great numbers, by procuring an act that no Dissenter should be allowed a seat in the assembly; and another for establishing the Church of England, erecting of Churches, and making provision for the maintenance of the clergy; which by the Dissenters were resented as act of highest oppression and tyranny.

They sent home an agent, to solicit redress from the Palatine Lord Granville; but were refused it. In 1705 they petitioned to the House of Lords, who condemned the above laws as repugnant to the charter, destructive of trade, and tending to ruin and depopulate the province. They were likewise condemned by the board of trade, to whom her Majesty the Queen referred the whole matter for examination. They also reported, that such acts were an abuse and forfeiture of the charter, and advised her Majesty to reassume the same. Upon this the acts were declared void, and orders given to the Attorney and Solicitor to prosecute by a que warrant; but the proprietor had interest enough to evade the prosecution. About this time several tribes of Indians entered into confederacy, and took up the hatchet against the English; they cut off several of the out settlements, and murdered many of the frontier inhabitants, but, being properly supplied with firearms, &c. they the savages several signal defeats, particularly one under the conduct of Colonel Barnwell, in North Carolina in 1712. The Indians continued the war till 1716, when, having assembled a large army, they marched towards the coasts; which Col. Craven, who was then Governor, having intelligence of collected what troops he could, and, marched against the Indians, who were posted near Combatee River, to the southward of Charles Town, where a bloody battle was sought, in which the Indians were entirely routed; and being far from the mountains, the place of their usual retreat, great numbers of them were cut off in their flight, and others taken prisoners and sold into slavery; some of the remains consented to a treaty, and others retired to a great distance.

In 1722, a general peace was concluded with all the Indians, including the Cherokees, then the most powerful nation of Indians in North America. About this time the coasts of this and the neighboring provinces were so infested with pirates, as to put a great stop to trade and navigation. To suppress these lawless miscreants, the province of South Carolina fitted out two sloops, the command of which was given to Col. Rhott, who after an engagement of some hours, took a pirate sloop, commanded by Major Stead Bennet, who with his abandoned crew was condemned and executed at Charles Town. But Blackbeard and others continued still to infest the coast for two or three years longer, especially about Carolina. One of these champions was so audacious, that, having taken a vessel off the bar of Charles Town, on board of which were several people of rank, bound to England, he detained them as hostages, sent his boats up to town, demanding a chest of medicines, and a supply of other necessaries, threatening, in case of refusal, and his boat was not suffered to return in safety, that he would put every one of the passengers to death; and such was the debility of the province at that time, that they were obliged to comply with his demands.

These misfortunes, added to their internal divisions and animosities, threw the colony into such confusion, that, upon seven of the proprietors consenting to sell out, the crown agreed to give each of them for his eighth share the sum of 2,500 pounds and a further sum of 5,000 pounds to be divided among them for the quitrents that were due; which agreement was confirmed by act of parliament, in 1726. But Lord Carteret, now Earl Granville, reserved his eighth part, both of the property and quitrents then in arrear, and all his rights, titles and privileges, as if no such act had passed; and hath since had his eighth part divided to him, which is about sixty miles on the sea coasts from North to South, adjoining to Virginia, and from the Atlantic Ocean east, to the South Sea west. As soon as the property and jurisdiction of this colony were thus vested in the crown, it was divided into two distinct provinces, each of which have a Governor, Council, &c. the form of their government being much the same as in common to all King's governments on the continent. There is however this difference in the two governments, namely, that North Carolina is divided into two counties, each of which hath a Sheriff and court of justice; but South Carolina they have an officer called the Provost Marshal, who acts as Sheriff of the whole province; and all courts of justice, excepting those of single justices of the peace are held at Charles Town; which regulations are attended with inconveniencies I have heard greatly complained of, as greatly increasing the expense of law suits to the parties, and often rendering the attendance of jurymen and witnesses difficult.

North Carolina

IS situated upon the sea coast about three hundred miles, and bounded east by the Atlantic Ocean, north by Virginia, west by the Appalachian Hills, and south by South Carolina. The coasts of this province are extremely broken by bays, creeks, and rivers, in the openings of which are many bars and shoals, which render the navigation difficult to strangers; there are, however, several safe and good harbours, and rivers are Roanoke or Albemarle River, Neuse River, and Cape Fear or Clarendon River; Upon which are situated the principle towns in the province, viz. Wilmington, on Cape Fear; Neuborn, on the Neuse, and Adenton, on Albemarle; at which three places their general court or assembly for enacting laws fit alternately.

But Wilmington is the largest town, and has much the largest trade of any in the province. The number of inhabitants in the whole province are computed to be about 70,000 whites, and 20,000 negroes. The country, for near a hundred miles from the sea, is flat, level, and sandy, the soil shallow and lean, being covered over with pitch and yellow pines; from which they manufacture prodigious quantities of tar, pitch, and turpentine, in which laborious and dirty business their droves of negroes are employed round the year. This soil will produce scarce anything but Indian corn, and not even that to any perfection without some kind of manure. There are some swamps of reeds in the southern parts, and on Cape Fear River marshes, which produce rice when properly cultivated; and on the north, towards Virginia, on which they raise tobacco. About a hundred miles in the country the land rises gradually to Appalachian Mountains, where the soil in some places is very good, and produces plenty of wheat and other grain; the timber being oak, intermixed with pine; they also here raise hemp and flax. And have some fruit. In this part of the province is plenty of wild game, especially deer; and the number of their cattle and swine is very great; some single planters owning a thousand head of dry cattle, which run in the woods all the year round, the calves being marked in spring, that each may know his own. These cattle they sold in herds, to manure the poor lands for Indian corn, which is the chief substance of the country people, as well as of the slaves, who grind or pound it, and boil it in milk.

The greatest number of inhabitants are in this westerly part of the province, as the soil here is most fruitful and pleasant. The air here is agreeable enough in winter, but very hot in summer; and the inhabitants are very subject to agues, fevers, cholicks, &c. There still remain some Indian towns in the province; part of the nation, called the Tuskararas, in the middle part; and Cotawpees in the southern, near the bounds of South Carolina; but they have met with very little disturbance from the Indians since they were made a King's government, till the late war with the Cherokees, in which their frontiers have suffered, with those of their neighbors. The principal export from this province are great quantities of pitch, tar and turpentine, to Europe and the neighboring provinces; to the northward, pork, beef, and corn, to the West Indies, droves of live cattle to Virginia, by which way they generally export their northern produce of tobacco.

The religious persuasion in this province are some of the Episcopalians; but a much greater number of the various sects of Dissenters.

SOUTH CAROLINA

THE bounds of **SOUTH CAROLINA** are very much reduced from their original extent; Georgia being taken off the southward, as far as the river Savanna, which runs in a curve round the south and west part of this province, out of North Carolina. The extent of this province upon the Atlantic Ocean to the east is upwards of 200 miles, to where Georgia and North Carolina meet. The face of this country, for sixty or seventy miles from the sea, is like that of North Carolina, low and level; then it gradually rises into hills. But the soil is vastly different, and infinitely better, and may be divided into pine land, oak land, swamps, and marshes. The pine land is by far of the greatest extent, and is a dry whitish soil, naturally producing a great variety of shrubs, and a coarse kind of grass, not very agreeable to cattle, unless in the meadows, or Savanna. Peaches grow here in great abundance, and the white mulberry tree, which is the food of silk worms. The oak land commonly lies in narrow slips between pine land, and swamps, creeks, or rivers; this soil is a blackish sand, producing several kinds of oak, bay, ash, laurel, boilsted, &c. On these lands are found the black mulberry, the American cherry, fox and cluster grapes, as they are called by the inhabitants, the former about the size of a small cherry, the latter of a white currant; these lands are the most esteemed, producing in great abundance rice, corn, &c.

The swamp lands are covered with Cyprus, or reeds; and when properly cultivated, are very productive rice. This province likewise abounds with cattle and swine, even beyond North Carolina; and its forests are stored with deer, beyond any of its neighbors, and many other kinds of wild game; nor are its rivers and sea destitute of fish and foul, common to the climate in which it lies; in short, this is a very rich and fertile province, and is peopled by many wealthy inhabitants, who live in great ease and splendor. The staple commodities are rice and indigo; of the former is annually exported upwards of 100,000 casks, which weigh from 510 to 600 lb. each; and of the latter, from 400,000 to 500,000 weight is annually exported; and great improvements are continually making in the cultivating and manufacturing of it. It is also found that the westerly part of this province produces wheat to great perfection, which no doubt will now be improved that way, being freed from the fear of those savages who lately infested their frontiers. They also raise flax, which, as their numbers increase, may likewise become a very considerable article to the province. This country also has a great variety of vegetables and fruits, as Spanish potatoes, pompions, melons, peas, beans, pears, peaches, pomegranates, oranges, &c. so that upon the whole it is calculated to be an exceeding rich and valuable territory, abounding not only with the necessaries, but many of the conveniencies of life, and having a great redundancy of both to spare to its neighbors. Its navigation is easy and safe upon the rivers Podee, Santee, and Savanna; from its different ports annually sail upwards of three hundred vessels laden with the produce of the country, among which may be reckoned deer skins as no inconsiderable article, the deer being so plenty, that the back inhabitants scarce need any other meat; and there is no doubt but that laborious animal the silk worm may be employed here to great advantage, here being hi natural food in great plenty. Some attempts that way have been made with good success, but not so as to render it very considerable. But, notwithstanding these delightful and inviting circumstances of this country, it has also its disagreeables; the air or climate is not so pleasant and healthy as could be wished for. The winters are short, and the spring delightful; but from May to September, and sometimes longer, it is exceedingly hot, with a thick sultry air in the forepart of the

SOUTH CAROLINA 103

day, which those who are not used to it can scarcely breath in; when the sun breaks out, it is with the most intense heat; the most sharp and heavy thunder and lightning frequency happen here, and very sudden changes and altercations in the weather, which render the summer season very unhealthy for strangers, and subject the inhabitants and natives themselves to fevers, dysenteries, and various distempers; and to all these the myriads of mosquitoes, which are enough to devour one during the summer season. It is difficult to sleep without a smoke in your bed chamber to expel them, or abate their impetuosity. You cannot other ways avoid being either stifled with the heat, or dinned and tormented by these animals.

Charles Town is the metropolis of this province, situated between two navigable rivers, Ashley on the west and south, and Cowper River on the East. The streets are at angles; those running east and west extend from one river to the other about a mile. Here are two very handsome churches built with brick, besides several other edifices for public worship belonging to the different sects of Dissenters. Near the center of the town is a neat market house; and near by it is the state house, which is a stately commodious brick building; in the neighborhood of the town are convenient barracks sufficient for a thousand men. There are in the town about one thousand dwelling houses, four thousand male inhabitants, and six thousand negro slaves. The number of inhabitants in the whole province is about 60,000 whites, and more than double the number of blacks. The religious persuasions here are much the same as in North Carolina.

the PROVINCE of GEORGIA

THIS province is about a hundred miles wide upon the sea, by which it is bounded eastward; southerly by East Florida; westerly, by the low lands of the Creeks, and partly by the south end of the Appalachian Mountains; and northerly by the river Savanna, which divides it from South Carolina. There are also several small but very fruitful islands included in this province, which lay off at a small distance from the continent.

This country was divided from South Carolina, and a settlement begun here, in 1732, in consequence of a representation made to his Majesty King George the Second, by some generous and compassionate Nobleman and Gentlemen, in behalf of distressed imprisoned debtors, the number of which at the time was very great in England. This territory lying waste and uninhabited, tho' capable of the most valuable improvements, these worthy persons formed a design at the same time to advance the public weal, and assist distressed individuals, and petitioned his Majesty for a grant of these lands, and that they might be incorporated as a trustees for settling the same; which being readily granted, a charitable subscription was set on foot for collecting benefactions, which succeeded so well, that they were enabled to relieve and send out one hundred persons, provided with all manner of necessaries, such as arms, tools for agriculture, and provisions for their supply for some time after their landing. Lieut. Colonel Oglethorpe, a truly zealous promoter of the design, was appointed to have the conduct and management of the intended settlement, which he began upon the river Savanna, about ten miles up, laying the foundation of the perfect town of Savanna.

This Gentleman prudently cultivated a friendship with the neighboring Indians, who not only suffered them peaceably and quietly to go on with their settlement, but often supplied them with provisions. The next spring they were reinforced by a number of new settlers, arriving with a supply of all kinds of necessaries; and great encouragement was given to this new settlement, not only by private benefactors, but several large sums granted by parliament; so that in 1734 the trustees were enabled to send out 491 persons upon the charity, besides several masters carrying with them 106 men servants at their own charge; in all amounting to 618 persons.

In 1735, a quantity of rice and raw silk, the produce of this province, was sent to England, which gave a new spring to charitable contributions in favor of it; and an act of parliament was passed, giving the same encouragement for the shipping of rice, the produce of Georgia, as was given to that of the produce of Carolina.

This province, by the wife, prudent and generous conduct of Mr. Oglethorpe, and others, continued to flourish and increase; the friendship of the Indians being secured, nothing material happened till 1752, when the trusties surrendered their charter to the crown; since which the Governor is appointed by his Britannic Majesty and the form of government the same that is common to all the King's governments.

The soil, air and produce of this province much resemble those of South Carolina; rice is said to grow better here than in South Carolina, which with corn and indigo may be esteemed at present its principal commodities. They have made some beginnings towards cultivating vines, and the making of raw silk; both which branches, if attended to, and improved upon, may hereafter become considerable, the climate and soil being very suitable for them, as hath been sufficiently proved by a variety of experiments.

the PROVINCE of GEORGIA 107

What has been said of the heat, unhealthiness, thunder and lightning at Carolina, may with the utmost propriety be said of them here, Georgia lying still more to the southward. The thunder and lightning often do very great damage to the planters, not only destroying their timber, houses, &c. but killing their slaves and cattle, in both of which they abound; and this province if possible, is more severely infested than South Carolina, with all manner of venomous and poisonous animals, from alligators of twelve feet long, to mites scarcely discernible by the eye; the alligators keep in fresh water rivers, and the savanna abound with them.

The principal towns in Georgia are, Savanna and Frederica. The former is the metropolis, and is very pleasantly situated; but is remarkable for nothing so much as the famous Orphan House, founded by Mr. Whitfield; but neither of this house, nor the charity, learning, and regulations of it, are any ways equal to the tumult and noise that have been made in the world about them; and, it is said, they are no ways equal to the contributions collected by that itinerating Gentleman for their support. The number of inhabitants in Georgia is about 8,000 whites, and 20,000 blacks. The inhabitants are a mixture of Episcopalians and Dissenters.

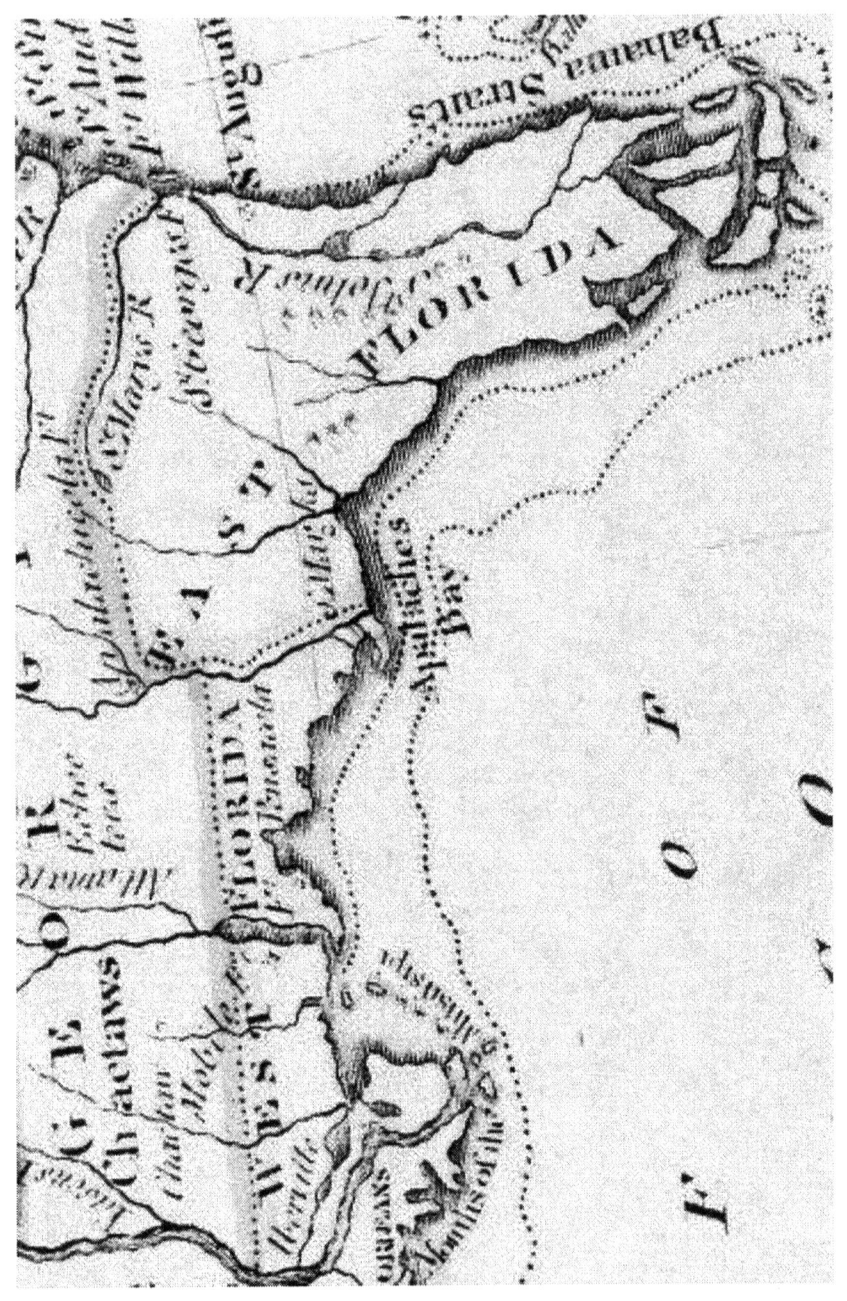

EAST and WEST FLORIDA

THE country south of Georgia, and between that and the Mississippi River, an extent of about 600 miles, was by the Spaniards called Florida, which name it still retains; but is now divided by the English into two provinces, viz. East and West Florida.

EAST FLORIDA is bounded north by Georgia, or St John's River, which divides them; eastwardly and southwardly, by the Gulf of Florida: southwest, by West Florida; and northwest, by the country of the Creek Indians.

The Spaniards attempted a settlement at St. Augustine in this province in 1512; however they were obliged to abandon this attempt, by reason of the savages, and other inconveniencies, they not being properly supplied with necessaries to go through with it. In 1565 they again took possession, and erected a fort called St. Augustine, which commanded a convenient harbour for their ships trading between Spain and America; but there being a constant war between the Spaniards and Creek Indians, greatly prevented the enlarging their settlements here. They maintained their garrison (through several attempts were made to reduce it by the Carolinians, and afterwards by General Ogethorpe) till the conclusion of the late war, when the garrison and the whole territory of Florida was ceded to the crown of Great Britain, by the treaty of Fontainebleau, in 1762. His Britannic Majesty being absolute Sovereign of the soil has the appointment of the Governors in both of the Floridas.

The soil of east Florida is not so good as that of Georgia in General; but the northerly part of it adjacent to Georgia is much like it, and may be improved to all the purposes that

Georgia is viz. for raising of corn, rice, indigo, silk, wine, &c. and again, in the west part of the province is some good land, capable of being improved to great advantage.

The center or cape of Florida is more sandy soil; however, there are some good settlements begun in this province, under the direction of Colonel Grant, the present Governor of it, and there is a prospect of its soon becoming a flourishing province; and as inhabitants are flocking to it from several countries in Europe, there is no doubt but in a short time it will be considerable.

Their exports at present are but small, the produce of their trade which the Indians being the chief they have to spare. As the country was three years since almost entirely uncultivated, and the number of inhabitants as yet but small, no great improvements and productions are at present to be expected; but, undoubtedly, this country is capable of producing rice, indigo, silk, wine, oil, and other valuable commodities in great abundance. As this country is new, it has great plenty of all kinds of wild game, common to the climate. The metropolis of this province is St. Augustine. The number of inhabitants, exclusive of his Majesty's troops garrisoned there, is, as I am told, about 2,000.

It may well be supposed, from its southerly situation, that the air and climate of this province is not more agreeable and healthy than that of Georgia, and that it is no less infested with poisonous and troublesome animals of various shapes and sizes.

WEST FLORIDA was seized upon by the French, who began a settlement in it at Pensacola, in 1720, and they enjoyed it till the before mentioned treaty of Fontainebleau in 1762, when this was ceded to and formed into a government by his Britannic Majesty. It is bounded, eastwardly, by East Florida; southwardly, by the Gulf of Mexico; westwardly, by the Mississippi River, and the lake St. Pier; and northwardly, by the country of the Chikitawa.

EAST and WEST FLORIDA

The principle town is Pensacola; and as many of the French, who inhabited here before the treaty, have chose to become British subjects for the sake of keeping their estates, this will contribute to the speedy peopling of this province, and no doubt render the settlements considerable very soon, especially as the land in this province is mostly very good, vastly preferable to the eastern province, its soil being capable of producing all the valuable commodities of rice, indigo, wine, oil, &c. in the greatest abundance; and its situation for trade is extremely good, having the River Mississippi for its western boundary.

They already carry on a very considerable trade with the Indians, and export great quantities of deer skins and furs. The French inhabitants here raise considerable quantities of rice, and build some vessels.

There are at present, as I am told, about 6,000 inhabitants in this province, which increase very fast, it being much more healthy and inviting than East Florida; especially the western parts upon the banks of the Mississippi, where it is said to be agreeable enough to English constitutions. In short, it is not to be doubted but that in a few years this will be a rich and flourishing province, nature having denied it nothing that is necessary to make it so.

The country, taken together, must appear to be no small part of the British empire, or at least of no small importance to it, if we consider its extent, the number of its inhabitants, the variety of its produce, and the great increase of trade and navigation thereby occasioned.

There are in this country no less than one million six hundred thousand British Subjects. From its several ports annually sail between three and four thousand vessels, laden with the produce of this, to other countries, the greatest part of which produce id given in exchange for goods of British manufacturing or importing; so that which but a few years ago was an inconsiderable rivulet, may now be compared a stream of wealth, flowing into the seat of the British empire, continually increasing, and growing more and more inexhaustible, and sending forth a greater variety of riches each year.

the
INTERIOR COUNTRY

THE Indians on the continent of North America are mostly retired from the sea coasts (where formerly they were very numerous) into the interior or westerly parts of the country, few of them being to be found within less than two or three hundred miles of the sea; for tho' many of them have been Christianized, and in some measure civilized, and parcels of land have been allotted to them in several of the British colonies, where they have been formed into societies; yet it is observable, that, in proportion as they lay by their savage customs, and conform to our methods of living, they dwindle away either because these methods are disagreeable and noxious to their constitutions, or else (which I am inclined to believe is the case) when settled among the English, they have greater opportunities of procuring spirituous liquors, of which they are generally, male and female, inordinately fond; and very little care has ever been taken to prevent those, who are inclined to take advantages of them in trade, for debauching them; by which means, where there were considerable settlements of them, a few years since, their name is now almost totally extinct. Those who still remain have mostly joined themselves to other nations in the interior country, who have generally erected their own towns upon the banks of lakes and rivers, where they enjoy sea coasts of their own, to all their purposes, as effectually as if they possessed the eastern shore of the continent.

The principal rivers in North America are, St. Lawrence, communicating with the sea at the Gulf of St Lawrence; the Mississippi, which flows into the Gulf of Mexico; and the Christinoux, which discharges itself into Hudson's Bay. There are great numbers of smaller note that join these in their course from the heights of the country to the sea.

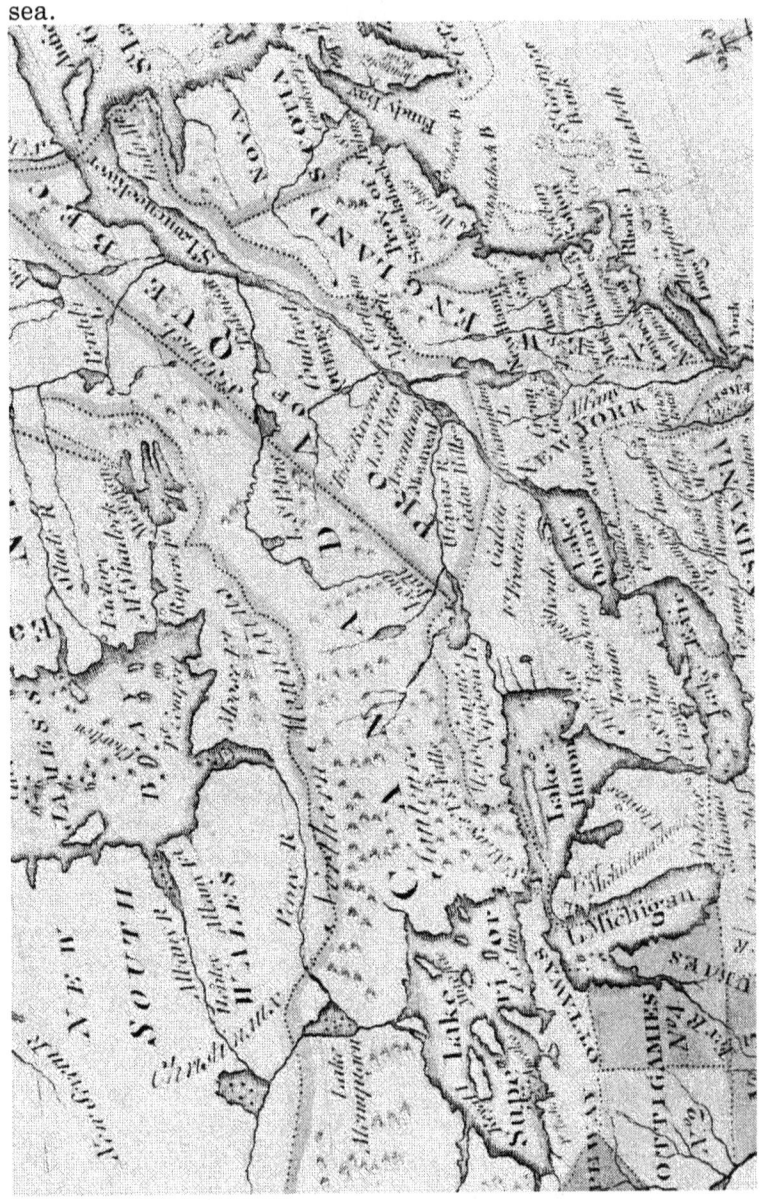

the RIVER ST. LAWRENCE

THIS river takes its rise upwards of two thousand miles from its mouth, at a lake called by the Indians Nippissong. (which in their language signifies a large body of water) situated northwest from Lake Superior, in latitude 52 degrees north. The northerly bank of this lake is a bog, or morass, that is near four hundred miles long from north east to southwest, and about one hundred and fifty miles broad. North of this bog is a ridge of mountains, extending from northeast to southwest, the whole length of the marshy country, and beyond it to the westward. These mountains are very high and steep, and are called by the Indians the Head of the Country, meaning thereby that they are situated In the center, and are the highest land on the continent of North America; which indeed seems to be the case; for, southeast of those rises the River St. Lawrence, having its course from thence southeasterly, northeast rises the River Christino. And runs northeasterly; and from the south, and southwest of these mountains rises the Mississippi, and runs southerly; so that by these rivers the continent is divided into many departments, as it were, from a center, which is the before mentioned mountains.

The Indians who inhabit round Lake Nippissong, the head of the River St. Lawrence, are called the Lake Indians or Nippislongs, and are in number about five or six thousand men. They chiefly live upon the west, south, and southeast of the lake, and on the islands in it, where the lands are tolerably good: the other parts being either marshy or mountains. Their country is of considerable extent, but of very difficult access; on which account they have never had but very little commerce with the English of French. They have no firearms, but hunt with bows and arrows. They have little or no war or connections with any other tribe of Indians, but live almost as independent as if they had a whole world to themselves. They sometimes go thro' the Christinaux country to Hudson's Bay, and purchase some clothing from the company; but their chief clothing is the produce of their own country, the skins of beasts. They never shave or cut the hair from their heads or any part of their bodies, on which account the other Indians esteem them a very savage and impolite herd, and don't chose any correspondence or connections with a people so rude and uncultivated. Their food is such as the lake and wild deserts afford them, such as deer, moose, bear, beaver, &c. and in the lake are great abundance a kind of wild maize or rice, which they make use of. They never pretend to plant or improve the land by labor.

From hence the River St. Lawrence runs through a rough, broken uninhabited country to Lake Superior, having in its course several falls perpendicular from a great height. The river is here a quarter of a mile wide; a rock extends straight across the stream, over which it falls with a noise that can be heard for several miles. Below these falls is great plenty of fish, especially trout, which are very large and good. At the entrance of the river into the lake is a town of Indians, called the Souties or Attawawas; which nation inhabit all along at the mouths of the rivers that fall into Lake Superior, and on the North of the lakes Michigan and Huron. They can raise about 12,000 fighting men. These Indians are more improved than the Nippissongs, having had considerable commerce with the French. They live in houses or huts that are built in the form of cones; the base is generally from sixteen to twenty feet wide, containing, commonly ten or twelve persons; the top of the cone is left open for about two feet, which aperture serves them both for a chimney and window, their fire being kindled in the center. To render these huts a defense against the cold, &c. they cover them with mats of rushes, which they have an art of weaving and placing in such a

the RIVER ST. LAWRENCE 117

manner as to render them warm and comfortable, and their appearance is very elegant, discovering the exactest order and good workmanship. When they remove for the sake of hunting, fishing, or any other convenience, they carry this external covering with them; by which means they are able, in a very short time, to erect new towns, with all the elegance and convenience of their old ones. They generally change their habitations in spring and autumn, spending the summer season upon the banks of the rivers and lakes, where they fish and raise corn, and the winter among the mountains, sometimes two or three hundred miles distant, for the sake of better hunting; and the food you meet with among them, is according to the season in which you visit them. They as yet, make but little use of spirituous liquors, nor do they manufacture any kind of drink, except the juice of the maple tree, of which they likewise make sugar; but live upon the simple gifts of nature when in health, and when sick, the woods and lakes furnish them with all the drugs they make use of; in the application of which some indeed are allowed to excel in skill, but ask no fee or reward for their trouble. And although there is such a thing as private property among them, which they transfer to one another, by way of bargain and exchange, and if taken out of the compass of their dealing, the aggressor is stigmatized, and punished with disdain; yet no individual or family is allowed to suffer by poverty, sickness or any misfortune, while their neighbors can supply their wants; and all this from the simple natural consideration, that they and their families are liable to the same unhappy circumstances they see their friends in.

At the north of Lake Superior is another tribe or division of these Indians, who call themselves the Bulls; these inhabit round the Bay, called by the French Merduoust, or the North-Bay. They differ not much from the Souties in their manners; they can raise about four thousand fighting men. They are originally of the Souties, or Attawawas nation, as evidently appears by the affinity between the two

Languages; for they can perfectly understand one another. The chief trade of these northern Indians is to Hudson's Bay, where they carry fur and ermine in great abundance, and exchange for blankets, arms, &c.

Lake Superior is upwards of two thousand miles in circumference, and very deep, excepting near the west end, where are several islands; and near where the river joins it is a large island, separated from the main by a straight of no more than five or six miles wide. The soil of this island is very good, and on it several Indian towns. The banks to the north, south and east are very high and steep in some places, being more than two hundred feet above the surface of the water, and almost perpendicular; so that it is very difficult landing at any place, except where the rivers fall in. On the north and east of this lake, the lands are broken and mountainous, intermixed with many small ponds and brooks of water; on the south and west of the lake, after you leave the banks, the country is level and good quite to the Mississippi, having large plains covered with tall grass; there being scarce any trees or other places, the oak, maple and locust trees are lofty and fair. There are some good islands in the north bay of this lake, of forty or fifty miles in length from north to south; but not near so wide.

The Indians in this territory certainly enjoy in the greatest plenty what they look upon to be the necessaries, and even the luxuries of life. Here are fish, fowl, and beasts of every size and kind, common to the climate, in the greatest abundance; nor do I see any reason why this should not become a rich and valuable country, should it ever be inhabited by a civilized people. It has rivers, it has a sea of its own, which make great amends for its inland situation, by facilitating trade and commerce from one part of the country to another, by cheap and easy conveyance; nor do the Indians entirely neglect this advantage, but make great use of canoes on the rivers and lakes; which vessels they make of the bark of birch, spruce, or elm; those made of the former are much the best and largest, and will carry from

the RIVER ST. LAWRENCE 119

four or five hundred to two thousand weight, and are a kind of vessel well suited to this country, being so light that a single Indian will carry one of a middling size, when they come to any cliff or cataract, till they think proper to take the water again.

The River St. Lawrence flows from Lake Superior to Lake Huron, upwards of one hundred and sixty miles, and joins it about twenty miles east of the Straights of Michlimakana. The stream here is generally very rapid, and has one considerable fall, round which the Indians are obliged to carry their canoes when they pass this way the land adjacent to the river between the two lakes is broken and hilly; but much of it is capable of being improved to good advantage. The timber is thick and lofty; and iron ore is here found in the greatest plenty, and it is said to be the best in America; and here are streams sufficient for all kinds of water works.

A little to the west of where the river joins Lake Huron, is a town of Souties, or Ottawawas Indians, who came here from the south of Lake Superior, their original country; and to the northeast of the lake is another town of the same Indians; and on the west side of the lake the Saganongs inhabit at the head of a bay called Saganong Bay. There are also several towns of Souties, or Ottawawas, upon the river flowing into the east and southeast of the lake. These Indians have much the same customs as those on Lake Superior.

The **LAKE HURON** is of a triangular form; one of the extremities points to the north east, where a considerable stream flows into it, called the Souties River, from which there is but a short carrying place to the Attawawas River, that joins St Lawrence River near Montreal. Another extremity points to the northwest, at the Straights of Michlimakana; the other to the south, where the River St. Lawrence issues out as from the point of a heart.

This Lake is about 900 miles in circumference; the country on the north and northwest of it is rocky and mountainous; on the southeast the land is low, and covered with tall timber, such as white pine, oak, walnut, ash, maple, &c. on the southwest, between Lake Huron and the Lake Michigan, the country is level and plain, having very few trees upon it of any kind; the soil is tolerably good.

This wide extended plain is covered with tall grass, among which are deer, elks, bears, raccoons, &c. in great plenty.

This country also abounds in a great variety of land and water fowls, and indeed seems to be destitute of nothing that is necessary to supply the natural wants of the human species.

The number of Indians that inhabit round Lake Huron is about 3,000 of which 600 are warriors, or fighting men.

LAKE MICIGAN is situated west from Lake Huron, and is very much of the same form, excepting that it is longer, extending further to the south. There is a communication between the two lake, by a straight called the Straight of Michlimakana. It is fifteen miles wide, and forty in length, running nearly east from the north of lake Michigan.

On the north end of Lake Michigan are several towns of Indians. At the south extremity the River St. Joseph flows into it, about 300 miles west of Detroit.

The country between the two lakes is level, and generally of an excellent soil, the timber lofty and fair. It is well watered by a variety of streams, running some into one lake, some into the other.

At the point adjoining Lake Michigan, and for five or six miles from it, south the land is sandy. Here stands our fort of Michlimakana, a good stockade, near twenty feet high. There are at this place, some French inhabitants, who come here for the sake of trading with the Indians, and for the trout fishery, which is here very valuable, the trout in these straights being exceeding plenty, and of an extraordinary size; some have been taken that weight upwards of fourscore pounds. The Indians from all the adjacent countries annually resort hither for the sake of these fish, notwithstanding which their numbers seem not to be diminished.

On the southeast side of Lake Michigan are some towns of the Souties, and at the south end live the Pottawattamies, which nation likewise inhabit the west side, and have several villages on that part of the lake.

The Indians round Lake Michigan amount to about 4,000 fighting men.

On the northwest part of Lake Michigan enters another straight from the Green Bay. This straight is about 40 miles wide, and 100 long, and in it are inhabited by the Pottawattamies and others by the Attawawas.

The **GREEN BAY** is of considerable extent. Into the north end of it flows a large river, that rises between Lake Superior and the Mississippi, which is called the river of Foxes, on which live a nation of Indians, Called the Fox Indians, whose number is less than 4 or 500 men; and further southward the county is inhabited by the Kekabouze, whose number is about 500 men.

The wide extended country upon this river, the Green Bay, and the straights from thence to Lake Michigan, is uniformly pleasant, the soil good and fertile, and wants nothing but civilized industrious inhabitants to render it truly delightful. It is at present well stored with a variety of wild game, the natural flocks and herds of its savage inhabitants.

The timber is tall, but not so thick as to prevent the growth of grass, which is here very luxuriant, it being generally five or six feet high, which sufficiently indicates the goodness of the soil. This invites hither the greatest plenty of deer, elks, buffaloes, wild cows, bears, beavers, &c. and it certainly appears a most desirable region, for the air is not less agreeable than the soil.

The winters are never severe, and great part of the year the country wears a verdure.

Here likewise grow spontaneous a great variety of grapes, which are agreeable enough to the palate, and doubtless might be manufactured to advantage. The Indians have learned, that the juice of these grapes will make glad the heart of man, making from them a kind of rough claret; but their want of knowledge how to manage it properly, no doubt, renders it vastly inferior to what it might be made. They deposit this liquor in empty rum kegs. This country also produces a kind of wild oats, or rice, which hath already been mentioned as growing upon Lake Superior and Nippissong; but here it grows in the greatest plenty in the shoal water, where a canoe may be loaded in a very short time; it grows two or three feet above the water. Its tussle resembles oats, but the kernel is more like rice. The Indians in this country raise Indian corn, and have horses in great plenty. Their cabins, or houses, are like those on Lake Superior, already described.

From this short account of the Lakes Huron and Michigan, the Green Bay, and the adjacent country, which I am certain is no ways exaggerated, nor even up to what will be found true of its beauty and territory, capable of rich improvements, and that the promoting a speedy settlement in it, and securing its advantageous posts, is even of a national importance. The French were so sensible of this, that they had advanced posts at the River St. Joseph, at the Green Bay, and at the Falls of St. Marie, at the time when Canada was ceded to the crown of Great Britain; all which have been since destroyed by the Indians; and the only post we now have in this part of the country is at Michlimakana, which is garrisoned with 100 men.

the RIVER ST. LAWRENCE

From the south point of Lake Huron, the River St. Lawrence runs easterly, inclining to the south for about eighty miles, where it flows into Lake Erie in its way, passing through Lake Sinclair, which is about twenty five miles above Lake Erie. The river at Lake Huron is about 500 yards wide, but much wider before it reaches the other Lake, there being several streams which join its on each side. The country on both sides the river is level and good, the timber is white pine, oak, maple, &c. of a good growth.

The river where it enters Lake Sinclair is divided into several branches, by which are formed five or six islands of various dimensions. The Lake Sinclair is nearly circular, and is about eighteen miles across. On the east side are large marshes of eight or ten miles extent from the water; and near the lower end, on the east side, a river enters the lower end, on the east side, a river enters it of a considerable bigness, from which by a short carrying place is an easy conveyance to Lake Ontario, used by the Indians who inhabit the banks of this river, who are a branch of the Souties or Attawawas. The land on the west side of the lake is also tolerably good, the timber chiefly beach and maple.

At the south side of the lake, where the river St. Lawrence leaves it, it suddenly divides into two branches, forming thereby an island of considerable extent, situated near the center of it; the easternmost branch keeps a pretty straight course, but that which turns to the westward forms a large bay, leaving a point of land between that and the lake called Long Point. From this bay it returns and joins the other branch, Forming the as foresaid island in the opening of the bay, and from thence keeps its course southwardly to Lake Erie; the land on each side of the river is level, good and fertile, quite from one lake to the other; on the eastward side of the river, a little below Lake Sinclair, is a town of the Attawawas, and further down towards Lake Erie, on the same side, is a town of Hurons; the river between these two lakes is near 800 yards wide; on the west side, below the before mentioned bay, is the fort of Detroit.

The French inhabitants here are settled on both sides of the river for about eight miles. When I took possession of the country soon after the surrender of Canada, they were about 2,500 in number, there being near 500 that bore arms (to whom I administered oaths of allegiance) and near 300 dwelling houses. Out fort here is built of stockades, is about twenty five feet high, and 1,200 yards in circumference; the land of this place is pleasant, and the land very good; the inhabitants raise wheat and other grain in abundance, and have plenty of cattle, but they enrich themselves chiefly by their trade with the Indians, which is here very large and lucrative.

Below Detroit, on the same side of the river, near where it enters Lake Erie, is an Indian town of the Pottawattamies, and below that the River Rouge, or the Red River, enters it opposite the west end of an Island, which divides the river St. Lawrence into two branches as it flows into the lake; there are also a little above this, two or three smaller islands, which are very beautiful; the river is here about two miles wide.

Lake Erie is 300 miles in length, from the southwest to the northeast, and eighty or ninety miles wide at the westerly end and about forty at the lower end, where it tapers off to seven or eight miles, before the river leaves it.

The river enters the lake at the northwest corner; and twenty or thirty miles south of this, at the west end of the lake, the river Miami flows into it. This river has an easy communication with the Ohio, by the river Wabash, there being no more than twelve miles land carriage between the two rivers*.

At the Southwest corner of Lake Erie, the Lake Sandusky communicates with it, by a strait of half a mile wide.

The Lake Sandusky is thirty miles in length, and eight or ten miles wide. Into the southwest corner of this lake the river Sandusky, or Huron, flows. Upon the banks of this

the RIVER ST. LAWRENCE 125

river, and round Lake Sandusky, the Huron Indians are settled in several different towns, in a very fertile country. This nation of Indians can raise about 6 or 700 fighting men. They differ something in their manners from the Souties, or any yet mentioned. They build regular framed houses, and cover them with bark. They are esteemed the richest Indians upon the whole continent, having not only horses in great abundance, but some black cattle and swine. They raise great quantities of corn, not only for their own use, but supply several other tribes. Who purchase this article from them.

Halfway between the river Miami and the Straits of Sandusky the river Huron flows in, on which there are some valuable springs.

The country of the Hurons extends 150 miles westwardly of the lake, and is 100 miles wide. The soil is not exceeded by any in this part of the world; the timber tall and fair; the rivers and lakes abound with a variety of fish, and here is the greatest plenty of wild water fowl of anywhere in the country. The woods abound with wild game. In a word, if peopled, and improved to advantage, would equal any of the British colonies on the sea coasts.

The country on the south side of Lake Erie is claimed by the Five Nation Indians, but not inhabited by them; they keep it for the sake of hunting. This also is a fine level country towards the south, from the lake, for several miles, having many streams flowing thro' it into the lake, from the high lands between this and the Ohio. Our fort at Presque Isle is upon this side of the lake, about 100 miles from the east end. From this fort is a carrying place of about twelve or fourteen miles to the French Creek, a branch of the Ohio. The country from this fort, down to where the river flows out of the lake, is somewhat rocky and hilly; up a river that flows into the east end of the lake, about ten miles south of where St. Lawrence leaves it, is a town of the Five Nation Indians. The country on the northward side of the lake is also level, the timber tall, but not near so good as on the south side. There are several streams which water this country, and flow into, or rather frequented by the Mississauga Indians, who tarry no longer in a place than wild game is plenty in it. They are a branch of the Souties, or Attawawas. Upon this side of the lake, and opposite to Presque Isle on the other side, is a peninsula called Long point, which extends into the lake 250 miles, and is six miles wide in the widest place, but where it joins the main not more than 100 yards.

There are also several islands in the lake, at the west end, which, tho' somewhat rocky, are good land, and might be improved to advantage. From the east end of Lake Erie, the river St. Lawrence runs northeasterly, inclining to the north, about fifty miles, to Lake Ontario. Nearly opposite to where it issues out of the lake, is a new fort, erected on the northerly side, called Fort Erie. Soon after the river forms itself, the current is rapid, on account of the rocks and falls in it, for about a mile; over which, notwithstanding, we work up vessels by the help of windlasses. A little below these ripples are several small islands, and at about six or seven miles distance the river is divided into two branches, by the southwest end of the Great island, which extends almost down to little Niagara Fort, and contains no less than 40,000 acres of land, which is very good. The country on both sides of the river to Little Niagara appears to be good and fruitful, and is wholly uninhabited.

Little Niagara Fort is nothing more than a stockade, and is about two miles distant from the easterly end of the Great Island, on the east side of the river.

Near this fort is a remarkable fall, or cataract, in the river, which deserves a particular description. This cataract is called the **Falls of Niagara**, which, in the language of the Five Nations, signifies a fall of water. The course of the river here is south-south-east, and about half a mile wide, where the rock crosses it, not in a direct line, but in the form

the RIVER ST. LAWRENCE 127

of a half moon. Above the fall is an island of about half a mile in length, the lower end of which comes to the edge of the fall. The current of the river above the island is quite slow; but as it approaches the island, and is divided by it, it runs more swiftly, and, before it comes to the fall, with such violence, as often throws the water to a considerable height, especially on the west side of the island, the whole stream appearing in a foam, for even here the descent is equal to the side of a pretty steep hill. When it comes to the perpendicular fall, which is a hundred and fifty feet, no words can express the consternation of travelers at first view, seeing so great a body of water falling, or rather violently thrown, from so great a height, upon the rocks below, from which it again rebounds to a very great height, appearing white as snow, being all converted into foam, thro' those repeated violent agitations. The noise of this fall is often heard at a distance of fifteen miles, and sometimes much further. The vapor arising from the fall may sometimes be seen at a great distance, appearing like a cloud, or pillar of smoke, and in it the appearance of a rainbow, whenever the sun and the position of the traveler favors. Many beasts and fowls here lose their lives, by attempting to swim or cross the stream in the rapids, and are found dashed in pieces below; and sometimes the Indians have met with the like fate, either carelessness or drunkenness. There are smaller falls in the river several miles below, which renders it unnavigable. The bank of the river, on the east side from the fall downwards, is 300 feet high, till you come to another fort of ours, distant from Little Niagara nine miles, and this length they are obliged to carry by land, on account of the rapids above and below the cataract. The land on the other side rises gradually, and perhaps no place in the world is frequented by such a number of eagles as this, invited hither by the carnage before mentioned, that is here made of deer, elks, bears, &c. on which they feed. The land on the west side of the river St. Lawrence, from this fort, or landing place, to Lake

Ontario, is owned by the Mississaugaus, and is tolerably good. The timber is chiefly chestnut. The easterly side is owned by the Five Nations, and is thinly timbered with lofty oaks, which, at first view, one would be apt to think were artificially transposed. The river enters Lake Ontario at the northwest corner, at which place is Niagara Fort, a handsome well built fortification, of considerable strength. A large bay shoot up from the entrance of the river westward. The form of this lake is oval, being about 260 miles in length, and 150 wide in the middle.

The country on the west and north of the lake, down to the river Toronto, which is about fifty miles, is very good.

At the west end of the river runs in, from which are carrying-places, both to Lake Sinclair and Lake Erie, or to rivers that flow into them.

The country upon the lake, between St. Lawrence and Toronto, is inhabited or owned by the Messissaugaus, and by the fair and lofty timber upon it, is a good soil. Here is likewise great plenty of grape vines. By one of the branches of the river Toronto is an easy communication with the rivers flowing into Lake Huron. Upwards of a hundred miles from Toronto, at the north easterly corner of the lake, the river Cataraqua flows into it; there are likewise several smaller streams between these, From Cataraqua is a carrying place to the Attawawas River, which joins St. Lawrence near Montreal. This country is also owned by the Mississaugaus, as far northward as Cataraqua; they likewise claim all the west side of **Lake Ontario**, and north of Lake Erie, but live a roving unsettled life, literally without any continuing city, or abiding habitation, as hath been already remarked of them. At the easterly corner of the lake flows in the river Oswego, where we have another fort erected, and a garrison kept up of a considerable force; this is about 200 miles from Niagara. The River Oswego rises from the Oneida Lake, which is about thirty miles in length. At the east end of the lake stands a royal block house, to

the RIVER ST. LAWRENCE

command a ferry over the Seneca River. The Oneida Lake is distant fifty or sixty miles from Lake Ontario. From the Oneida is an easy communication with the Mohawk (and consequently with Hudson's) River, by the way of Wood Creek.

This country upon the Lake, between Oswego and St. Lawrence, is level and good for several miles from the lake.

This country is owned by the Five Nations. There are several rivers flowing through it to the lake; the most considerable is the River Sable, which joins the lake eighty or ninety miles east of Niagara and rises near a branch of the Ohio. There are several falls upon it, and one higher than the Falls of Niagara. The stream is about 200 feet wide for a great way up. It is very much concealed from the traveler, as he passes it on the Lake, by an island situated before the mouth of it, About 150 miles up this river, are those remarkable springs, greatly esteemed by the Indians as a remedy for almost every disease; they are called oil springs, on account of an oily substance that issues forth with the water, and rises upon the surface of it. The Indians use these springs for consumption, asthmas, and various internal disorders, by drinking the water; and for rheumatic pains, strains, dislocations, &c. by bathing, with great success. A little further eastward flow in the river Arundicat and Chinesee.

In the rivers round Lake Ontario are salmon in great plenty during the summer season; and at the entrance of the river St. Lawrence are, during the winter season, an abundance of a kind of fish, called white fish, which seems to be peculiar to this place, there being none such any where else in America, excepting some few at Long Point nor can I learn that any such are to be seen in Europe. In summer they disappear, and are supposed to lie during that season in deep water, out of soundings. They are about the size of shad; and very agreeable to the palate. Here is great plenty of water fowl, and game of all kinds common to the climate.

In a word, the country round this lake is pleasant, and apparently fertile, and capable of valuable improvements.

The Five Nations have their towns, not adjacent to the lake, but at some distance from it, and mostly upon the rivers that flow into it. The river St. Lawrence takes its leave of Lake Ontario at the northeast corner of it. Near the lake it is ten or twelve miles wide, having several islands in it, on one of which, the most northerly, at the head of the rifts, is a small fortress, erected by the French, and now kept up by us. A little south of this island a considerable stream flows in, which rises near Hudson's River, and is called Oswegotchy, and has frequent falls after you ascend it forty or fifty miles down from the lake. Here the river grows narrower.

From Lake Ontario to the Cedars, the present western boundary of the province of Quebec, is about eighty miles, and from thence to Lake St. Francis, which may be called the next stage of St. Lawrence, is nearly the same distance.

On the south side of the river, at the bottom of the rifts, is a small village of Five Nations, and another on the same side towards Montreal.

In the river, and in the Lake St. Francis, are several islands, which are mostly settled by the French, belonging to the province of Québec.

The country on both sides the river is tolerably good, and is capable of supporting many thousands of inhabitants. On the northerly side of the Lake St. Francis, the Attawawas River flows in and joins the river St. Lawrence, as hath been already mentioned. The Attawawas rise east of Lake Superior, from a small lake, where is an Indian tribe, who call themselves Roundocks; and opposite to the northeast corner of Lake Huron is another small lake, which the Indians call Nippissong (in their language a lake.) The stream which flows from it is joined by another of some considerable bigness, that rises from several small lakes

the RIVER ST. LAWRENCE 131

among the mountains. Where these two rivers unite are many islands, which render the passage very difficult to find. From the head of the west branch of the river, there is but a short portage to another that falls into Lake Huron, by which way our traders sometimes carry their goods to and from the Indians in this part of the country; but this way is much more difficult than that of Niagara, being obstructed by a great number of falls, round which they are obliged to carry their goods and canoes.

There is another very small settlement of the Roundocks upon the river, between the islands and its junction, after a south east course, is by three different channels; one flows into the Lake St. Francis, and the other two form the Island of Jesus, north of Montreal, and meet and unite with the river St. Lawrence, at the east end of the Island Montreal.

The country upon the banks of this river is broken, and not very good, till you come near the river St. Lawrence. The timber is chiefly white pine, of a tall growth. The winters are cold, and subject to deep snows, much more so than the main river, as we have traced it down. There is, however, great plenty of beaver in this country, and the river, for some way up, abounds with salmon, which two articles are the chief substance of the Indians residing here, who pretend not to keep any animals but dogs. But after all, even this country, by a civilized industrious people, might be rendered fertile and delightful, beyond many in the world that are now very populous.

There are several settlements, of the St. John's, Cape Sable, and several other tribes of Indians, upon the streams falling into St. Lawrence from the south, between that and Nova Scotia, and round the gulf of St. Lawrence, between that and the Bay of Fundy, and the coasts of the province of Maine, whose chief subsistence is the wild game of the country, for they raise but little corn, and keep no cattle.

There are also some Indians upon the north side of St. Lawrence, near Québec, called Hurons, but none of any great account. About thirty or forty miles below Québec, a river flows in from the north, that heads near Hudson's Bay, or James River, on the banks of which live some other tribes of the Roundocks; but all the Indians of the lakes excepting the Hurons and Five Nations, have an affinity in their language, and appear to be originally from the same nation.

From this account of the country upon the river St. Lawrence, above what is now called the province of Québec, there seems a prospect in future, not only of a flourishing province, but a rich and great kingdom, exceeding in Europe, and exceeded by few, if any, in the fertility of its soil, or the salubrity of its air, and in its present uncultivated state, abounding with many of the necessaries and conveniencies of life; and tho' it has no open communication with the sea, yet great amends are made for this defect by its numerous lakes and streams running to and from them, by which there is an easy communication from one part of the country to another, almost through the whole. In a word, there is no part of North America at present discovered, excepting that on the Mississippi that appears better worth settling, improving, and defending than this. It is in my many respects preferable to any of the colonies on the sea coasts, exclusive of their improvements, and has a larger territory than any six of them.

This country, if any in America, will always have the advantage of the fur and peltry trade, on account of its large lakes, and the extended uninhabitable country to the northward of it, both of which will tend to keep up that valuable and lucrative branch of commerce here to the end of time.

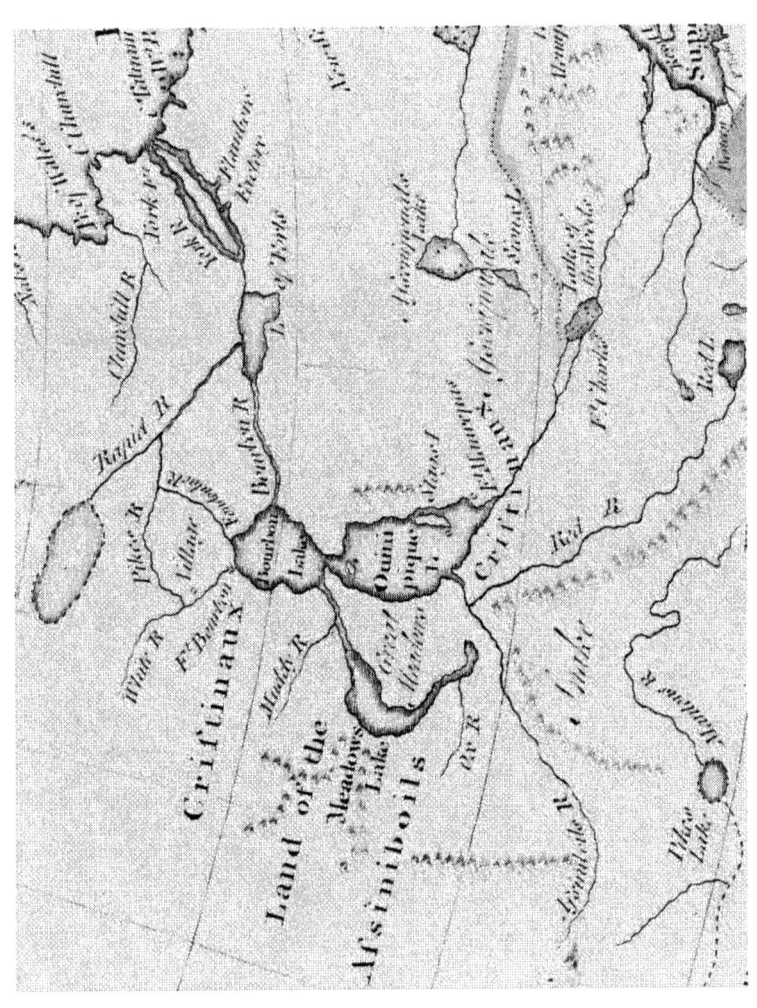

the RIVER CHRISTINO

THIS River is so called from the Indians, the Christinaux, who posses the country adjacent to it. Its highest source is, as high as hath been mentioned, at the northeast of the central mountains, called by the Indians the Head of the country.

It rises in several streams, all which bend their course towards Hudson's Bay, and fall in with each other at different places, till, in the course of about 150 miles from the source, they all unite, by which confluence a very large bay is formed, round which a tribe or division of Christinaux lives. As you advance further down the river, there are some few lakes, but none large, or deserving of a particular description.

There are several small streams which flow in on each side of the river, from a low boggy country, by which its waters are increased, till finally it discharges itself into Hudson's Bay, near 200 miles north of York Fort, and about 500 miles from the before mentioned mountains.

The country adjacent to this river is vastly inferior to that on the lakes and the river St. Lawrence, as may well be supposed from its northerly situation, it lying between 55 and 60 degrees of north latitude. The winter are long and severe, the snow deep, and sometimes on the earth great part of the year. The soil is cold and barren, and scarcely capable of any valuable improvements; so that this country, excepting its wild game, seems to have very little to invite any of the human species into it, or to subsist them upon when they visit it.

Near the bay, and for a considerable way up the river, the land id high, and so thickly covered with spruce, hemlock, &c. that it is difficult to travel thro' it without being entangled, but nearer the mountains the soil is better. The timber here is beech and maple, tho' some of it is low and marshy, and covered with hemlock, where it is unfit for grain or fruit of any kind. There are in the river some kinds of fish, and the beaver are taken in great abundance, and some ermines, elks, moose, bears, &c. There is also an animal resembling the moose, but much smaller, which deems peculiar to this country. The fish and wild came are the sole subsistence of the inhabitants, for they raise no kind of grain, nor do they keep any animals except dogs.

The number of Indian warriors in this country is supposed to be about 2,000. They generally cover their houses, or huts, with the skins of wild beasts, and not only make them warm and secure, but according to their taste, very neat and elegant. These Indians have very near the same language with those on the lakes, and north of the river St. Lawrence; according to their own history, or account of themselves, they all came round from the north into this country. Tho' the only history they have is a verbal one, handed down from the father to son, they however pretend in this way to have an exact account for many generations back; and certain it is, that tho' they neglect the education of their children in almost every other respect, they are extremely careful and solicitous in this way to acquaint them with the history or story of their ancestors.

Further northward still, are some other rivers that flow into Hudson's Bay; but the country adjacent to them being still more northerly, is inferior, if possible, to that of the Christinaux. The Indians who inhabit it are much the same; only this seems observable in general, that the further north you travel on the American continent, the more savage and unimproved the nations appear to be.

These Indians, and even the Christinaux, rarely travel south of the central mountains; some few of the latter have been known to visit our traders at Lake Huron and Michigan; but their chief trade is to Hudson's Bay, to which

the RIVER CHRISTINO 137

place the Nippissongs, round the lake of that name, sometimes carry their furs thro' the country of the Christinaux. It is possible that all these northern Indians are only different tribes or divisions of the same nation, their manners, language, and customs, being similar.

From James's Bay, and along the coasts of Labrador, the country is inhabited, or rather frequented by a nation called the Eskimaux, who are a wandering unsettled generation, roving in large parties during the summer season, and come quite from Hudson's Bay northward to the Straits of Belle Isle, which they sometimes cross over to Newfoundland.

These Indians give a different account of themselves from the others; they say, that they crossed Hudson's Straits into this country; from which it is supposed, by some, that they came from Tartary; and, indeed, their customs and methods of living favor this opinion. Not withstanding this prodigious extent of country over which they are not very numerous being but about 4,000 men. They subsist chiefly upon animals which they take out of these northern seas, such as whales, seals, and the like; and eat or rather devour and gormandize raw flesh, when they cannot with conveniency cook it.

These Indians clothe themselves with the furs and skins of such animals as they take in the woods and waters; during the winter season they abide in caverns underground, and feed chiefly on whale oil and blubber, unless raw flesh chance to be thrown in their way. They travel chiefly by water, in a kind of canoes peculiar to themselves, which are so contrived as to ride through almost any storm that can happen; for in case of bad weather, they can lace or enclose themselves in and keep dry, while the canoe is rolled over and over without damage. These canoes are made of skins stretched over a frame of small timber, very near in the shape of the bark canoes, and then lined or ceiled over with skins; which lining or ceiling is sewed fast

138   A CONCISE ACCOUNT OF

to the keel and the gunwale, and then left so long as to meet and lace together in the middle, if there should be occasion.

In the center between the two ends is a partition which divides the canoe into two apartments; in one of which, when a storm threatens, or there is danger of over setting, one person is stationed, being laced up tight round the body with the aforesaid lining, and, in case of oversetting, it is his business to right again, while the other for there is never more or less than two in a canoe when they venture far) is securely enclosed at the other end. They sometimes venture several leagues to sea in those canoes in pursuit of whales, seals &c.

Their chief trade is to our fort on James's Bay, and with such vessels as frequent their coast for the sake of trading with them.

The Indians on the Island of Newfoundland appear to be much the same sort with those last mentioned.

They are called Micmacks; they both bear the greatest resemblance of the wild beasts of any savages that we are acquainted with; on which account they are considered and hated as a barbarous and beastly people by all other Indians in the neighborhood, who have but little commerce or correspondence with them.

the RIVER CHRISTINO

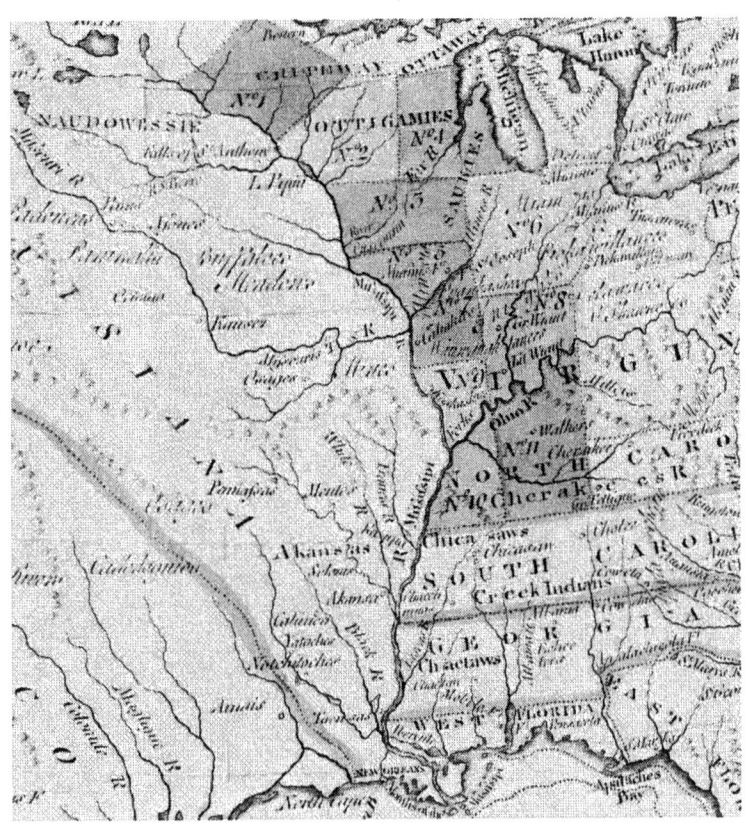

the MISSISSIPPI

THIS river takes its rise at the southerly part of the central mountains, upwards of 3,000 miles, as the river runs from its mouth at the Gulf of Mexico. Its highest source is a lake of considerable bigness, opposite to or northwest of which is a notch or opening in the mountain, from which a large stream flows to the lake, carrying with it a red sulphureous substance, by which the water is discolored; on which account this is called Red Lake. It has a fine fertile country on the southeast parts of it.

The course of the Mississippi from which the Red Lake is nearly southwest for upwards of two hundred miles, where it is joined by a smaller stream from the westward, and its course is turned nearly southeast for more than three hundred miles, where it is joined by the Muddy River, and before that by another not so large, flowing to its northeast. The Muddy River rises from the south of the central mountains, out of the large bog before mentioned, and runs south, inclining to the west, till it meets the Mississippi coming from the northwest, after which junction the head to this place is generally pretty rapid, and has frequent and large falls; but the country on both sides of the river, and of the branches that flow into it, is exceeding fine and good. The timber lofty, but thin; the plains large, and fertile. The air and climate, even quite to the head, moderate and agreeable. The winters short, and rarely severe; though in the same latitude, further eastward, they are quite the reverse, it being observable, that, after you pass the Great Lakes and Hudson's Bay to the westward, there is a very perceptible change in the air, and the further you travel westward, the more mild and temperate it grows, and the country is more agreeable and fertile. The lakes and rivers here abound with fish, and the wild oats or rice before mentioned grows here in great plenty. On the wide extended plains are multitude of wild cattle, which much resemble the Spanish cattle. There is also great plenty of deer, elks, buffaloes, and some beavers, hares, and panthers, and wild fowls in abundance, especially turkeys, and another kind of wood fowl, much larger, and almost as tall as a man; these run very swift, but cannot fly, unless it be from some eminence, and a small space of time. This fruitful country is at present inhabited by a nation of Indians, called by the others, the White Indians, on account of their complexion, they being much the fairest Indians on the continent; they have however Indian eyes, and a certain guilty Jewish cast with them. This nation is very numerous, being able to raise between 20 and 30,000 fighting men.

They use no weapons but bows and arrows, tomahawks, and a kind of wooden pikes, for which reason they often suffer greatly from the eastern Indians, who have the use of firearms, and frequently visit the White Indians on the banks of the easterly branch, and kill or captivate them in great numbers; such as fall alive into their hands, they generally sell for slaves. These Indians live in large towns, and have commodious houses; they raise Indian corn, tame the wild cows, and use both their milk and flesh; they keep great numbers of dogs, and are very dexterous in hunting. They have little or no commerce with any nation that we at present are acquainted with. From the confluence of the Muddy River the course of the Mississippi is nearly south for two hundred miles (the current strong, and in some places rapid) where it is joined by a large stream from the west, which rises four hundred miles from the central mountains, and its waters chiefly spring from the north and northeasterly part of the Missouri Ridge, a chain, or rather a double chain of mountains, so called, by which reach over towards the Isthmus of Darien. This is called by the Indians the Bloody River, on account of the long and bloody wars which have happened between the Indians here and those to the eastward.

the MISSISSIPPI 143

Four hundred miles further down, another river flows in from the northwest, which rises near the Bloody River. The two last mentioned rivers are both inhabited by the Illinois Indians, who likewise posses the western banks of the Mississippi for several hundred miles, and till you come to the river that flows into it from the east, and rises near the Green Bay, having but a short carrying place to the stream that empties into that, and to another that falls into Lake Michigan, near Fort St. Joseph. The country adjacent to this branch of the Mississippi was once inhabited by the Illinois Indians; but they are now mostly retired to the west side of the Mississippi; some few still remain at the mouth of the aforesaid river, where the French had likewise begun a settlement, which extended for fifty miles along the Mississippi, and a considerable way up the River Illinois. There they raised excellent tobacco, and carried on a large trade with the Indians up the Mississippi, and on the lakes. They also raise here excellent wheat, barley, and other grains. They had formerly a good fort here, well garrisoned, for the protection of the colony; but, since this place was ceded to the crown of Great Britain, the French have erected a garrison on the other side of the river, where the greatest part of the inhabitants have retired; those of them who were Germans (of which there is a considerable number) chose to tarry on this side, and become British subjects. Near this fort is a village of Indians; but their largest settlement is on the west side, some miles above this, where they have a town containing near 8,000 men; and above that, about a hundred miles, is another. They have also many large towns on the branches that fall into the river from the west.

Thee Indians live very well, have comfortable houses, make great use of horses; their country abounds with deer, elks, buffaloes; &c. In some parts of this country the timber is fair and tall; in other parts, for several hundred miles, there is scarce any timber to be found. The soil and air are pleasant and agreeable.

About a hundred and fifty, or two hundred miles below, where the Illinois flows into the Mississippi on the east side, the **MISSOURI** joins it on the west. This river takes its rise from the east and southeast of the before mentioned Missouri ridge of mountains in many different streams, for near 1,000 miles on this side, which unite with each other at different places, and, after an easterly and southerly course of near 2,000 miles, as the river runs, it flows into the Mississippi.

There is perhaps no finer country in the world than that which lies extended on each side of the Missouri, whether we regard the salubrity of the air, or the fertility of the soil. There are in this country near a thousand Indian towns. The inhabitants on this river are called the Missouri Indians, who are able to raise great numbers of fighting men; and have much the same customs and manners as the Illinois, who are likewise very numerous. The goodness of the country which they both inhabit, if possible, must render life agreeable and easy to persons who, like them, are content with having the demands of nature answered, without endeavoring to increase these demands by any studied refinements in dress, equipage, or the modes of living. In short, these people, of any upon earth, seem blessed in this world; here is health and joy, peace and plenty; care and anxiety, ambition and the love of gold, and every uneasy passion, seem banished from this happy region, at least to a greater degree than in almost any other part of the world.

The River Mississippi, after being joined by the Missouri, is about six miles wide, and continues its course southerly; it is joined by no considerable stream after this for between two or three hundred miles, where the Ohio flows into it, and makes a large addition to its waters.

The country, on each side the Mississippi to this place, is much the same as that already described; but the climate is something warmer, and is owned by the Tweeghtwees, or

Yeahtanees, on the east side down to the Ohio, and eastwardly from the Mississippi as far as the Wabash.

The **RIVER OHIO** rises in several branches, one of which is near Presque Isle, on Lake Ontario and within six miles of the lake; about ten miles down this branch stands Fort Du Beaus, from which place it is navigable for canoes and small boats quite to the mouth. The course of this branch is southerly for seventy or eighty miles below Fort Du Beaus, where we had another fort called Venango*. About twenty miles above this last fort, on the banks of the stream, are several little towns of the Mingo Indians, who removed hither from Hudson's River, and now belong to those called the Five Nation Indians. Opposite to Venango Fort this branch is joined by another large one from the northeast, which rises in the country of the Five Nations, and renders the navigation still more feasible; and about halfway from thence to Fort Pitt, there is another which joins it from the northeast, and after their meeting it is called the Ohio River, till you come to Fort Pitt, where it is joined by the Monogahela, which rises from the west side of the Allegana Mountains in a great number of small streams, that unite at no great distance from the mountain, and from this stream.

* *Venango, Fort Du Beauf, and Presque Isle, were all destroyed by the Indians in 1763; and whether they are rebuilt, I cannot tell.*

Fort Pitt is a regular well built fortress, is kept in good order, and well garrisoned; it is a very necessary post for the protection of our frontiers; indeed none is more so in this country, excepting Niagara and Detroit. Fort Pitt stands upon the point of land between the rivers Monongahela and Ohio.

From this the general course of the river is west, inclining to the south for near a thousand miles, as the river runs, where it joins the Mississippi. At Fort Pitt it is a mile wide, but grows much wider before its junction with the Mississippi, being joined by several streams in its, course thither. As the Muskegon and **WABASH** from the north, and the Tennessee from the south. The Muskegon rises toward Lake Erie, and the Wabash near the river Miami, the carrying place between them being but twelve miles long, at which place was formerly a small fort; at the distance of a hundred and fifty miles or two hundred miles from this fort, another stream flows, that rises near the Illinois, and from which the Indians have a carrying place to it, and often pass this way, when bound to Detroit from the Illinois country; where the stream joins the Wabash, stood the Yeahtanees Fort, so called from Indians of that name, inhabiting the adjacent country.

The Moskongom River rises near one that flows into Lake Erie, about forty miles east of Sandusky; and, by a short carrying place, the Indians convey their commodities this way to the Ohio. As far down the Ohio as the River Wabash, the country on each side is claimed by the Five Nations; the Shawanees at present inhabit it, who can raise about three hundred fighting men; and further eastward, towards Lake Erie, live the Delawares, who can raise about five hundred fighting men.

These are in league with the FIVE NATIONS, and hold their lands under them, and are sometimes called the Sixth Nation; and all together, since this alliance, which is of some years standing, have the general appellation of six Nation Indians.

The Mohawks are the head or chief nation, and preserve a superiority over the others.

The Delewares and Shawanees raise but little corn, and subsist themselves chiefly by their hunting, at which they are very expert; their houses, tho' covered with bark, are very comfortable.

West of the Wabash, as far as the Mississippi south, to where the Ohio joins it, and north to the heads of the Wabash and Yeahtanees Rivers, the country is owned by the

the MISSISSIPPI 147

Tweeghtwees or Yeahtanees Indians, who can furnish out about two thousand fighting men. Their chief settlements are at the heads of the before mentioned rivers.

Too much can hardly be said in commendation of this wide extended country upon the Ohio, the Wabash, Yeahtanees, and other streams flowing into it.

The country between the lakes and the junction of the Ohio and Mississippi, for several hundred miles, and all the country between Fort St. Joseph and the Green Bay, and between Detroit and the Illinois, and even much further north than Detroit, is level, the soil excellent, the climate healthy and agreeable, and the winters moderate and short. Its natural productions are numerous and valuable. It is sufficiently, but not too thickly timbered; what there is, is tall and fair, and fit for any common use. In short, no country in this quarter, if any in the world, is capable of larger or richer improvements than this.

There is a good coal mine near fort Pitt, made use of by the garrison for fuel; and what is still more in commendation of this country, it is extremely well watered by springs and riverlets, and has an easy communication with the whole world from the mouth of the Mississippi, and with great part of the interior country of North America, by its several branches, the Wabash, Missouri, Yeahtanees, the Ohio, &c. and with the Great Lakes by the way of Presque Isle, where a small expense would turn the waters of the lakes into the Ohio. At present the portage is but at a small distance, and the land level. Indeed such is the situation of this country, that, at or near the junction of the Ohio and Mississippi, in my opinion, within a century or two, it would be the largest city in the world, for hither flow, and here center, the exports of all the country upon the Mississippi, the Wabash, the Tennessee, the Great Lakes, &c. &c. The imports to this country will be most easy and natural up the rivers St. Lawrence and Hudson, by way of Montreal and Albany, and up the Delaware to Philadelphia, and from thence over the mountains, the navigation up the Mississippi being difficult.

Below the river Ohio, on the east side of the Mississippi, down to its mouth, the country is owned and inhabited by the Chicketaws for near two hundred miles to the eastward. This nation can raise 10,000 fighting men. The soil of this country is sandy, and not so good as that above described; however it produces rice and indigo to good perfection, of which the French have made sufficient proof. The Chicketaws generally live in large towns, their chief settlements are not far from the banks of the Ohio, on the streams that flow into it from the east.

Their houses are not very elegant; however they have the art of making them tight, which necessity obliges them to do, to secure themselves against flies, which are here very troublesome at some seasons of the year. They keep cows, hogs, and horses, the latter in great abundance. They raise plenty of corn, beans, potatoes, &c. but have very little game, except deer.

The Cherokees inhabit the southwest end of the Appalachian Mountains, from the head of the Tennessee River, which flows into the Ohio, about a hundred miles before its junction with the Mississippi. The extent of their country from northeast to southwest is about four hundred miles, and about two hundred miles wide. It is very mountainous and broken, and difficult of access any way. They live in as good as any savage on the continent. They build their houses with wood, and seal them with clay mixed with straw, so as to render them tight and comfortable. They have many small towns dispersed among the mountains on the branches of the rivers Tennessee and Savanna. They have great plenty of horses, some black cattle, and many swine. They raise corn in abundance, and fence in their fields (which no other Indians do); they also keep poultry, and have orchards of peach trees. They likewise attend to gardening. They are very famous for hunting, and their country abounds with deer, bears, and some elks and turkeys in great plenty in the fertile valleys between the mountains.

The Cherokees can raise about 2,000 fighting men. The Tennessee is wholly uninhabited below the mountains to where it joins the Ohio; but the country upon it is claimed by the Chickasaws, a brave warlike people, who have but one town, situated on a plain by a small creek that rises about thirty miles south of the Tennessee. Their town is picqueted in, and fortified with a fort. They build their houses much in the same form as the Chickasaws. They raise corn in great abundance, and have large droves of horses, some black cattle and swine. They can raise about five hundred fighting men.

The Creek Indians live southwest of the Cherokees, partly between them and the Chickasaws, St. Augustine and Georgia, and have a level country. They live in the same manner, and have the same commodities as the Chickasaws and Cherokees, and can raise about 2,000 fighting men. All the country of the Creeks is infested with alligators and snakes of a very large size, and flies, that at certain seasons are very great torment to them.

From the Missouri down to the west side of the Mississippi the soil is good, till you come near the mouth of it. The French have a settlement (a little above where the Ohio flows in) on the west side; about a hundred miles, from whence to New Orleans the country is better settled. The produce of this country is rice, Indian corn, and some wheat. The Island of Orleans is a beautiful and fertile spot of ground, on which the French have a considerable town. The number of French in this province is about 100,000. The Negroes are very numerous. The soil towards the south is well adapted to wheat. The number of inhabitants increases very fast, and will in a short time become a large colony; and, if possessed by those ambitious neighbors the French, will be capable of creating fresh troubles to the British

150 A CONCISE ACCOUNT OF

subjects in America; especially as in it and adjacent to it are great numbers of savages, who are still in their interest, and whom they never yet failed to excite and encourage to acts of hostility, even in times of peace. On the west side of the Mississippi, adjoining to the French settlements, are the Chataw Indians; their country is much like that already described, opposite to it on the east side, and their manners and methods of living the same as the Chickasaws and Cherokees.

CUSTOMS, MANNERS, &c.
of the INDIANS

HAVING thus endeavored to give a sketch of the interior country of North America, so far as I have any knowledge or intelligence concerning it, I will now more particularly, but briefly, mention the customs, manners and connections of the Indians who inhabit there.

Those of them who have any concerns or commerce with the English, are such as inhabit from the east side of the Mississippi to the south side of the River Christino; and among all the nations and tribes in this vast extent of country, those called the Five Nation Indians stand distinguished, and are deserving of the first notice. They are dreaded and revered by all the others for their superior understanding, activity and valor in war, in which constant practice renders them expert, they being in almost continual wars with one nation or other, and sometimes with several together. Their customs, manners, and modes of dress, are adopted by many of the other tribes as near as possible. In short, those Indians are generally among the other nations esteemed the politest and best bred who the nearest resemble these. Their most northern settlement is a town called Chockonawago, on the south of the River St. Lawrence, opposite to Montreal; but their largest settlements are between Lake Ontario and the provinces of New York and Pennsylvania, or the heads of the Mohawk, Tennessee, Oneida and Onondaga Rivers. They claim all the country south of the River St. Lawrence to the Ohio, and down the Ohio to the Wabash, from the mouth of the Wabash to the bounds of Virginia; westerly, to the Lakes Ontario and Erie, and the River Miami; their eastern boundaries are Lake Champlain, and the British colonies. When the English first settled in America, they could raise

15,000 fighting men; but now including the Delawares and Shawnees, they do not amount to more than between three or four thousand, having been thus reduced by the incessant wars they have maintained with the other Indians, and with the French, in Canada.

The Mohawks were formerly the most numerous tribe amongst them, but now they are the smallest; however, they still preserve a superiority and authority over the rest, as the most honorable nation, and consulted and appealed to by the others in all great emergencies. About 100 years ago they destroyed the greatest part of the Hurons, who then lived on the south side of Lake Ontario, and the remains fled to the French in Canada for protection; but the greatest part have since returned to their own country again, and live by permission from the Five Nations, on the lands at the west end of Lake Erie. They also took prisoners the whole nation of the Shawnees, who lived upon the Wabash, and afterwards, by the mediation of Mr. Penn, at the first settlement of Pennsylvania, gave them liberty to settle in the westerly parts of that province; but obliged them, as a badge of their cowardice, to wear petticoats for a long time; they gave them, however, the appellation of cousins, and allowed them to claim kindred with the Five Nations, as their uncles. They conquered the Delawares about the same time, and brought them into the like subjection; and also the Mickanders, or Mohegons, that lived on the banks of Hudson's River. They suffered the two last mentioned nations to live in any uninhabited part of their southern territory but the latter, upon condition of paying them an annual tribute. They also conquered several tribes upon the frontiers of New England. Some nations to this day are not allowed to appear ornamented with paint at any general meeting or congress where the Five Nations attend, that being an express article in the capitulations. They have been inveterate enemies to the French ever since their first settling in Canada, and are almost the only Indians within many hundred miles, that have been proof against us; but

CUSTOMS, MANNERS, &c of the INDIANS 153

the greatest part of them have maintained their integrity, and been our steadfast friends and faithful allies.

They once burnt a great part of the city of Montreal, and put the French into great consternation; they also conquered most of the Abnaques, or Eastern Indians. They now maintain a constant war with the Cherokees, Creeks, and Chickasaws, and many of their young men are annually employed that way; others of them go against the Missouri; and in short, they sometimes carry their hostilities almost as far south as the isthmus of Darien; but they have long lived in peace with the Indians on the lakes, and with the Tweeghtwees, those two nations being too near, and well provided, to retaliate any affront they may offer them.

The Indians do not want for natural good sense and ingenuity, many of them discovering a great capacity for any art or science, liberal or mechanical. Their imaginations are so strong, and their memories so retentive, that when they have once been at a place, let it be ever so distant, or obscure, they will readily find it again. The Indians about Nova Scotia and the Gulf of St. Lawrence have frequently passed over to the Labrador, which is thirty or forty leagues, without a compass, and have landed at the very spot they at first intended; and even in dark cloudy weather they will direct their course by land with great exactness; but this they do by observing the bark and boughs of trees, the north side, in this country, being always mossy, and the boughs on the south side the largest.

It is also observable, that you will rarely find among the Indians a person that is any way deformed, or that is deprived of any sense, or decrepit in any limb, notwithstanding the little care taken about the mother in the time of her pregnancy, the neglect the infant is treated with when born, and the fatigues the youth is obliged to suffer; yet generally they are of a hale, robust, and firm constitution; but spirituous liquors, of which they are insatiably fond, and the women as well as the men, have already surprisingly lessened their numbers, and will, in all probability, in one century more nearly clear the country of them.

Indeed the mothers, in their way, take great care of their children, and are extremely fond of them. They seldom wean them till they are two years old, or more, and carry them on their backs till the burden grows quite insupportable to them. When they leave the cradle they are very much at liberty to go when and where they please; they are however careful to instruct them early in the use of arms, especially the bow, and are often recounting to them the exploits and great achievements of their ancestors, in order to inspire them with great and noble sentiments, and lead them on to brave and heroic actions. They introduce them very young into their public councils, and make them acquainted with the most important affairs and transactions, which accustoms them to secrecy, gives them a composed and manly air, inspires them with emulation, and makes them bold and enterprising. They seldom chastise their children; when they are young, they say because they are not endowed with reason to guide them right, otherwise they would not do wrong; when they are more advanced in life, they say, because they are capable of judging, and ought to be masters of their own actions, and are not accountable to any one. These maxims are carried so far that parents sometimes suffer themselves to the abused by their children; and in the same way they will excuse any ill treatment they meet with from a drunken man; Should we blame or punish him, say they, when he does not know what he does, or has not his reason? When a mother sees her daughter act amiss, she falls into tears, and upon the other's taking notice of it, and enquiring the cause, she replies, because you so and so dishonor me; which kind of admonition seldom fails of the desired effect. The Indians do not always enter into a formal obligation of marriage, but take companions for a longer or shorter time, as they please; the children which

CUSTOMS, MANNERS, &c of the I N D I A N S   155

spring from hence lie under no disgrace, but enjoy all the privileges of lawfully begotten children.

The Indian men are remarkable for their idleness, upon which they seem to value themselves, saying, that to labor would be degrading them, and belongs only to the women; that they are formed only for war, hunting, and fishing; tho' it is their province to make and prepare everything requisite for these exercises, as their arms for hunting, lines for fishing, and to make canoes, to build and repair their houses; but so profoundly lazy are they, that they often make their women assist in these, besides attending al domestic affairs, and agriculture.

Most of the Indians are possessed of a surprising patience and equanimity of mind, and a command of every passion, except revenge, beyond what philosophers or Christians usually attain to. You may see them bearing the most sudden and unexpected misfortunes with calmness and composure of mind, without a word, or change of countenance; even a prisoner, who knows not where his captivity may end, or whether he may not in a few hours be put to a most cruel death, never loses a moment's sleep on this account, and eats and drinks with as much cheerfulness as those into whose hands he has fallen.

Their resolution and courage under sickness and pain is truly surprising. A young woman will be in labor a whole day without uttering one groan or cry; should she betray such a weakness, they would immediately say, that she was unworthy to be a mother, and that her offspring could not fail of being cowards. Nothing is more common than to see persons, young and old of both sexes, supporting themselves with such constancy under the greatest pains and calamities, that even when under those shocking tortures which prisoners are frequently put to, they will not only make themselves cheerful, but provoke and irritate their tormentors with most cutting reproaches.

Another thing remarkable among these people, who put on at all times a savage, cruel appearance, is, that those of the same nation, or that are in alliance, behave to each other with an high degree of complaisance and good nature.

Those advanced in years are rarely treated disrespectfully by the younger; and if any quarrels happen, they never make use of oaths, or any indecent expressions, or call one another by hard names; but, at the same time, no duration can put a period to their revenge; it is often a legacy transferred from generation to generation, and left as bequest from father to son, till an opportunity offers of taking ample satisfaction, perhaps in the third or fourth generation from those who first did the injury. They are not, however, strangers to the utility and pleasures of friendship, for each of them, at a certain age, makes choice of some one near about their own age, to be their most intimate and bosom friend; and those two enter into mutual engagements, and are obliged to brave any danger, and run any risk to assist and support each other; and this attachment is carried so far, as even to overcome the fears of death, as they look upon it to be only a temporary separation, and that they shall meet and be united in friendship in the other world, never to be separated more, and imagine they shall need one another's assistance there as well as here.

There is no nation of Indians but seem to have some sense of a Deity, and kind of religion among them; but this is so various, so perplexed and confused, that it is difficult to describe it very minutely. Their ideas of the nature and attributes of the Deity are very obscure, and some of them absurd; but they all acknowledge him to be the creator and master of the world; but how the world was created they know not, and of course have various conjectures about it. Some of them imagine that men were first rained down from the clouds, and that brute animals descended with them. They seem to have some idea of angels, or spirits of an higher and more excellent nature than man; to these they attribute a kind of immensity, supposing them to be

CUSTOMS, MANNERS, &c of the I N D I A N S   157

everywhere present, and are frequently invoking them, imagining they hear them, and act, or endeavor to act, agreeable to their desires. They likewise hold an evil spirit, or demon, who, say they, is always inclined to mischief, and bears great sway in the creation; and it is this later that is the principal object of their adorations and devotions; they generally address him by way of deprecation, most heartily beseeching him to do them no harm, but avert evils from them: the other they address by way of petition, supposing him to be propitious, and ever inclined to do them good; that he would bestow blessings upon them, and prevent the demon or evil spirit from hurting them; and to merit or produce the protection of the good spirit, they imagine it necessary to distinguish themselves; and that, in the first place, they must become good warriors, expert hunters, and steady marksmen.

The Indians depend much upon their dreams, and really believe that they dream the whole history of their future life, or what it may be collected from in their youth, for which reason they make dreaming a kind of religious ceremony when they come to sufficient years, which is thus performed. They besmear their face all over with black paint, and fast for two days, in which time they expect the good genius, or propitious spirit will appear, or manifest himself to him in some shape or other in his dreams. The effect which this long fast must naturally occasion in the brain of a young person must without doubt be considerable; and the parents, and other old people, take care, during the operation, that the dreams they have in the night be faithfully reported next morning. In favor to particular constitutions, they sometimes curtail this fast to a shorter term than is generally judged necessary; and this good genius, or propitious spirit, being the subject of the person's waking thoughts, becomes also the subject of his dreams, and every phantom of their sleep is regarded as a figure of the genius, whether it be bird, beast, fish, or tree, or anything else, animate or inanimate, and is particularly respected by them all their lives after. When any person of more distinguished parts then ordinary rises up among them, they suppose him naturally inspired, or actuated by this propitious spirit, and have an uncommon regard and veneration for him on that account, supposing him to receive intimations and intelligences from the good genius, or some of his agents. Religious impostures are not less frequent among the Indians of America, than among the Christians of Europe: and some of them are very successful in persuading the multitude that they are filled with a divine enthusiasm, and a kind of inspiration, few knowing better how to act their part in this sacred jungle than they.

They often persuade the people that they have revelations of future events, and that they are authorized to command them to pursue such and such measures. They not only prescribe laws and rules, and persuade the populace to believe them; but undertake to unfold the mysteries of religion and a future state, to solve and interpret all their dreams and visions, &c. They represent the other world as a place abounding with an inexhaustible plenty of everything desirable, and that they shall enjoy the most full and exquisite gratification of all their senses; and hence it is, no doubt, that the Indians meet death with such indifference and composure of mind, no Indian being in the least dismayed at the news that he has but a few hours or minutes to live; but with the greatest intrepidity sees himself upon the brink of being separated from terrestrial things, and with spirit and composure harangues those who are around him, and thus a father leaves his dying advice to his children, and takes a formal leave of all his friends.

The Indians generally bury their dead with great decency, and erect monuments over their graves. They deposit in the grave such things as the deceased had made the greatest use of, and been most attached to; as pipes, tobacco, bows, arrows, &c. that they may not be in want of anything when he comes to the other country. The mothers mourn for their children a long time, and the neighbors

CUSTOMS, MANNERS, &c of the I N D I A N S   159

make presents to the bereaved father, which he retaliates by giving them a feast.

The Indian feasts whether at a funeral, a triumph, a visit, or whatever the occasion be, are very simple and inartful. The savage does not mortify his friend with a splendid appearance, but makes him cheerful by dividing his riches with him, and values not spending the fruits of a whole season's toil, to convince him that he is welcome; may, thinks himself happy in having such an opportunity to oblige him. The guest is sure to be treated with an unaffected gravity and complaisance, and that he shall not be the subject of whispering ridicule and banter while present, nor of cruel remarks when departed; enjoy among more civilized nations. Nor is a servile regard paid to the distinctions of high and low, rich and poor, noble and ignoble, so as to lessen the spirit and pleasure of conversation, when the company happens to be made up of a mixture of these.

The Indians being both of a very active and revengeful disposition, they are easily induced at any time to make wars, and seldom refuse to engage when solicited by their allies; very often the most trifling provocations rouse them to arms, and prove the occasions of bloodshed and murder; their petty private quarrels being often decided this way, and expeditions of this kind may be undertaken without the knowledge or consent of war. These private excursions are winked at, excused, and encouraged, as means of keeping their young men alert, and of acquainting them with the discipline and exercises of war. And indeed these petty wars seem necessary, since their laws and penalties are insufficient to restrain them within the bounds of reason and common justice, and are a poor security of private property against the insults and depredations of anyone; but when war becomes a national affair, it is entered upon with great deliberation and solemnity, and prosecuted with the utmost secrecy, diligence and attention, both in making preparations and in carrying their schemes into execution.

Their method of declaring war is very solemn and pompous, attended with many ceremonies of terror. In the first place, they call an assembly of the Sachems and Chief Warriors, to deliberate upon the affair, and determine upon matters, how, when, and in what manner it shall be entered upon and prosecuted, &c. In which general congress, among the northern Indians and the Five Nations, the women have a voice as well as the men. When they are assembled, the President or chief Sachem proposes the affair they have met to consult upon, and, taking up the hatchet (which lies with him) says, Who among you will go and fight against such a nation? Who among you will go and bring captives from thence, to replace our deceased friends, that our wrongs may be avenged, and our name and honor maintained as long as rivers flow, grass grows, or the sun and moon endure? He having thus said; one of the principal warriors rises, and harangues the whole assembly; and then address himself to the young men, and inquires, who among them will go along with him and fight their enemies? When they generally rise, one after another, and fall in behind him, while he walks round the circle or parade, till he is joined by a sufficient number.

Generally at such a congress they have a deer or some beast roasted whole; and each of them, as they consent to go to war, cuts of a piece and eats, saying, this way will I devour our enemies, naming the nation they are going to attack. All that choose, having performed this ceremony, and thereby solemnly engaged to behave with fidelity and as a good warrior, the dance begins, and they sing the war song; the matter of which relates to their own skill, courage and dexterity in fighting, and to the manner in which they will vanquish and extirpate their enemies; all which is expressed in the strongest and most pathetic manner, and with a tone of terror. So great is the eloquence or influence of their women in these consultations, that the final result very much depends on them. If any one of these nations, in conjunction with the Chiefs, has a mind to excite one, who

CUSTOMS, MANNERS, &c of the I N D I A N S 161

does not immediately depend upon them, to take part in the war, either to appease the manes of the husband, son, or near relation, or to take prisoners, to supply the place of such as have died in her family, or are in captivity, the presents, by the hands of some truly young warrior, a string of wampum to the person whose help she solicits; which invitation seldom fails of its desired effect. And when they solicit the alliance, offensive or defensive, of a whole nation, they feed an ambassy with a large belt of wampum, and a bloody hatchet, inviting them to come and drink the blood of their enemies.

The wampum made use of upon these and other occasions, before their acquaintance with the Europeans, was nothing but small shells, which they picked up by the sea coasts and on the banks of the lakes; and now it is nothing but a kind of cylindrical beads, made of shells white and black, which are esteemed among them as silver and gold are among us. The black they call the most valuable, and both together are their greatest riches and ornaments; these among them answering all the ends that money among us. They have the art of stringing, twisting, and interweaving these into their belts, collars, blankets, mogasons, &c. in ten thousand different sizes, forms and figures, so as to be ornaments for every part of dress, and expressive to them of all their important transactions. They dye the wampum of various colors and shades, and mix and dispose them with great ingenuity and order, and so as to be significant among themselves of almost anything they please; so that by these their records are kept, and their thoughts communicated to one another, as ours are by writing.

The belts that pass from one nation to another, in all treaties, declarations, and important transactions, are carefully preserved in the palaces or cabins of their Chiefs, and serve, not only as a kind of record or history, but as a public treasure. It must, however, be an affair of national importance in which they use collars or belts, it being looked upon as a very great abuse and absurdity to use them on trifling occasions. Nor is the calumet or pipe of peace of less importance, or less revered among them in many transactions, relative both to war and peace. The bowl of this pipe is made of a kind of soft red stone, which is easily wrought and hollowed out; the stem is of cane, elder, or some kind of light wood, painted with different colors, and decorated with the heads, tails, and feathers of the most beautiful birds, &c. The use of the calumet is, to smoke either tobacco, or some bark leaf, or herb, which they often use instead of it, when they enter into an alliance, or on any serious occasion, or solemn engagement; this being among them the most sacred oath that can be taken, the violation of which is esteemed most infamous, and deserving of severe punishment from heaven. When they threat of war, the whole pipe and all its ornaments are red; sometimes it is red only on one side, and by the disposition of the feathers, &c. one acquainted with their customs will know, at first sight, what the nation who presents it intends or desires. Smoking the calumet is also a religious ceremony upon some occasions, and in all treaties is considered as a witness between the parties; or rather as an instrument by which they invoke the Sun and Moon to witness their sincerity, and to be, as it were, guarantees of the treaty between them. This custom of the Indians, tho' to appearance somewhat ridiculous, is not without its reasons; for, they finding smoking tended to disperse the vapors of the brain, to raise the spirits and qualify them for thinking and judging properly, introduced it into their councils, where, after their resolves, the pipe was considered as a seal of their decrees, and as a pledge of their performance thereof, it was sent to those they were consulting an alliance or treaty with; so that smoking among them in the same pipe is equivalent to our drinking together, and out of the same cup.

 The size and decorations of their calumets are commonly proportioned to the quality of the persons they are presented

CUSTOMS, MANNERS, &c of the I N D I A N S   163

to, and the esteem or regard they for them, and also to the importance of the occasion.

Another instrument of great esteem and importance among them is the tomahawk. This is an ancient weapon universally used by them in war, before they were taught the use of iron and steel; since which hatchets have been substituted in lieu of them. But this instrument still retains its use and importance in public transactions, and, like the pipe, is often very significant. This weapon is formed much like a hatchet, having a long stem or handle; the head is a round ball or knob of solid wood well enough calculated to knock men's brains out, which on the other side of the stem terminates to a point where the edge would be, if made a hatchet, which point is set a little hooking or coming towards the stem; and near the center, where the stem or handle pierces the head, another point projects forward of a considerable length, which serves to thrust like a spear, or pike pole.

The tomahawk likewise is ornamental with feathers and paintings, disposed and variegated in many significant forms, according to the occasion and end for which it is used; and on it they keep journals of their marches, and most important and noted occurrences, in a kind of hieroglyphics. When the Council is called to deliberate on war, the tomahawk is painted all over red, and when the council sits it is laid down by the chief; and if war is concluded upon, the captain of the young warriors takes it up, and with it in his hands dances and sings the war song, as before mentioned; when the council is over, this hatchet, or some other of the kind, is sent by the hands of some warrior to every tribe concerned, and with it he presents a belt of wampum and delivers his message, throwing the hatchet on the ground, which is taken up by one of their most expert warriors, if they choose to join; if not, they return it, and with a belt of their wampum, suitable to the occasion.

Every nation or tribe have their distinguishing ensigns or coats of arms, which is generally some beast, bird, or fish. Thus among the Five Nations are the bear, otter, wolf, tortoise and eagle; and by these names the tribes are generally distinguished, and they have the shapes of animals curiously pricked and painted on several parts of their bodies; and when they march through the woods, generally at every encampment they cut the figure of their arms on trees, especially if it be from a successful campaign, that travelers that way may know they have been there, recording also, in their way, the number of scalps or prisoners they have taken.

Their military dress has something in it very romantic and terrible, especially the cut off their hair, and the paintings and decorations they make use of. They cut of, or pull out all of their hair, excepting a spot about the size of two English crowns near the crown of their heads, their beards and eyebrows they totally destroy. The lock left upon their head is divided into several parcels, each of which is stiffened and adorned with wampum, beads, and feathers of various shapes and hues, and the whole twisted, turned, and connected together, till it takes a form much resembling the modern Pompadour upon the top of their heads. Their heads are painted red down to the eyebrows, and sprinkled over with white down. The gristles of their ears are split almost quite round, and then distended with wire or splinters, so as to meet and tie together in the nape of their necks. These also are hung with ornaments, and have generally the figure of some bird or beast drawn upon them. Their noses are likewise bored, and hung with trinkets of beads, and their faces painted with diverse colors, which are so disposed as to make an awful appearance. Their breasts are adorned with a gorget, or medal of brass, copper, or some other metal; and that horrid weapon the scalping knife hangs by a string which goes round their necks.

Thus attired, and equipped with the other amour they make use of, and war like stores, they march forth, singing

CUSTOMS, MANNERS, &c of the INDIANS   165

the war song, till they lose sight of the castle or village from which they marched, and are generally followed by their women for some considerable space, who assist them in carrying their baggage, whether by land or water, but commonly return before they proceed to any action.

When a small party goes out, they seldom have more than one commander, i.e. if the number does not exceed ten, which is one of their companies; if there be twenty, they have two commanders; if forty, four, &c. and when it comes to 100 or upwards, a general is appointed over the others, not properly to command, but to give his opinion and advise, which they make no scruple to disregard, if it does not happen to tally with their own; however, it is very rare that the directions of the general are disregarded, especially if countenanced and supported by the advice of old men, which seems to be the highest authority both in the state and army amongst them.

The generalissimo, or commander in chief, as well as military, among all the Indians to the northward, who speak the Roundock dialect, is elective, which election is attended with many ceremonies of singing and dancing; and the chief, when chosen, never fails making a panegyric upon the person to whom he succeeds.

The Indians have no stated rules of discipline, or fixed methods of prosecuting a war; they make their attacks in as many different ways as there are occasions on which they make them, but generally in a very secret, skulking, underhand manner, in flying parties that are equipped for the purpose, with a thin light dress, generally consisting of nothing more than a shirt, stockings, and mogasons, and sometimes almost naked.

The weapons used by those who have commerce with the English and French, are commonly a firelock, hatchet, and scalping knife; the others use bows, tomahawks, pikes, &c.

In any considerable party of Indians you will generally find a great number of headmen, or chiefs, because they give that title to all who ever commanded; but all these are subordinate to the commander of the party, who, after all, is a general without any real authority, and governs by advise only, not by orders; for he can neither reward nor punish, and every private man has a right to return home when he pleases, without assigning any reason for it; or any number may leave the main body, and carry on a private expedition, when, how, and where they please, and are never called to account for so doing.

The commander, every morning, harangues the detachment under his command, and gives his advice for the conduct of affairs during the day. If he wants to detach a party for reconnoitering, or on occasion he proposes the matter, and gives his opinion how, when, where, what number, &c. and of his measures. So greatly are the savages influenced by a sense of honor, and the love of their country, that coercive penal laws are needless to restrain and govern them upon these occasions; but then it should be observed, that the qualifications indispensably necessary to recommend a person to the chief command among them, are that he must be fortunate, brave, and disinterested; and no wonder that they cheerfully obey a person in whom they firmly believe that all these qualifications are united; to which may be added, that of secrecy in all his operations; in which art they greatly excel, their designs being seldom known to any but themselves, till they are upon the point of being executed.

The chiefs seldom speak much themselves at general meetings, or public assemblies, counting it beneath their dignity to utter their own sentiments upon these occasions in an audible manner; they therefore instruct them with a person to declare for them, who is called their speaker or orator, there being one of this profession in every tribe and town; and their manner of speaking is generally natural and easy, their words strong and expressive, their style truly

CUSTOMS, MANNERS, &c of the I N D I A N S   167

laconic, nothing being said but what is to the purpose, either to inform the judgment, or raise such passions, as the subject matter naturally excites.

Those who profess oratory, make it their business to be thoroughly acquainted with the subject they are to speak upon, and have the whole matter and method well fixed in their memories beforehand, that they may be at no loss what to say, or how to express themselves; and tho' they hold no regular parliaments, or courts of justice, yet they have frequent opportunities to display their talents this way, they being almost constantly busied in making fresh, or renewing former treaties, in tenders of their services, in solicitations, in addresses on the birth, death, or advancement of some great person, &c.

In their private petty debates, not only the orators, but every person is heard who chooses to intermediate in it; and generally, if one has given a present to a sachem for his vote one way or other, he is pretty sure to have it, for they seldom fail of performing engagements of this kind, which renders justice in the redress of private grievances very precarious.

But this is not attended with so bad consequences as one would imagine, for their contentions of a private nature are few, and are generally compromised by the interposition of friends.

Avarice, and a desire to accumulate those great disturbers of the peace of society, are unknown to them; they are neither prompted by ambition, nor actuated by the love of gold; and the distinctions of rich and poor, high and low, noble and ignorant, do not so far take place among them as to create the least uneasiness to, or excite the refreshment of any individual; the brave and deserving, let their families or circumstances be what they will, are sure to be esteemed and rewarded. In short, the great and fundamental principals of their policy are, that every man is naturally free and independent; that no one or more on Earth has any right to deprive him of his freedom and independency, and that nothing can be a compensation for the loss of it.

When the Indians return from a successful campaign, they manage their march so as not to approach their village till towards the evening. When night comes on they send two or three forwards to acquaint their chief, and the whole village, with the most material circumstances of the campaign. At daylight, next morning, they clothe their prisoners with new clothes, adorn their heads with feathers, paint their faces with various colors, and put into their hands a white staff or wand, tasseled round with the tails of deer. When this is done, the war captain or commander in this expedition sets up a cry, and gives as many holloos or yells as he has taken scalps and prisoners, and the whole village assembles at the water side, if there be one near. As soon as the warriors appear, four or five of their young men, well clothed, get into a canoe, if they came by water, or otherwise march by land; the two first carry each a calumet, and go singing to search the prisoners, whom they lead in triumph to the cabin where they are to receive their doom. It is the prerogative of the owner of this cabin to determine their fate, tho' very often it is left to some women, who has lost her husband, brother, or son, in the war; and, when this is the case, she generally adopts him into the place of the deceased, and saves his life.

The prisoner, after having been presented, has victuals immediately given him to eat, and while he is at this repast a consultation is held; and if it be resolved to save the prisoner's life, two young men unite him, and, taking him by the hands, lead him directly to the cabin of the person into whose family he is to be adopted. But if the sentence be death, the whole village set up the death holloo or cry, and the execution is no longer deferred than till they can make the necessary preparations for it. They first strip the person who is to suffer from head to foot, and, fixing two posts in the ground, they fasten to them two pieces crossways, one about two feet from the ground, the other about five or six

CUSTOMS, MANNERS, &c of the I N D I A N S   169

feet higher; they then oblige the unhappy victim to mount upon the lower cross piece, to which they tie his legs a little asunder. His hands are extended, and tied to the angles formed by the upper cross piece; and in this posture they burn him all over the body, sometimes first daubing him with pitch. The whole village, men, women, and children, assemble round him, and every one has a right to torture him in what manner they please, and as long as there is life in him. If none of the bystanders are inclined to lengthen out his torments, he is not kept long in pain, but is either shot to death with arrows, or enclosed with dry bark, to which they set fire; they then leave him on the frame, and in the evening run from cabin to cabin, and strike with small twigs their furniture, the walls and roofs of their cabins, to prevent his spirit from remaining there to take vengeance for the evils committed on his body; the remainder of the day, and the night following, is spent in rejoicings.

The above in their most usual method of executing prisoners; but sometimes they fasten them to a single stake, and build a fire round them; and at other times they gash and cut off the fingers, toes, &c. of their prisoners, joint by joint; and at other times they scald them to death. They often kill their prisoners on the spot where they take them, or in their escaping, or when they find it inconvenient to carry them further. But having been unsuccessful, things wear quite a different face; they then return and enter the village without ceremony by day, with grief and melancholy in their countenances, keeping a profound silence; or if they have sustained any loss, they enter in the evening, giving the death hoop, and naming those they have lost, either by sickness or by the enemy. The village being assembled, they sit down with their heads covered, and all weep together, without speaking a single word for some considerable time. When this silence is over, they begin to lament aloud for their mourning among them for several days.

Such in general are the manners and customs of the Indians called the Five Nations, which in the main agree to those of all the Indians with whom we have some things peculiar to themselves. Among the Hurons (who are called fathers by the Five Nations, and who are doubtless of the same nation) the dignity of Chief is hereditary, and the succession is in the female line; so that, on the death of the Chief, it is not his son, but his sister's son, that succeeds him, and in default of him, his nearest relation in the female line; and in case this whole line should be extinct, the most noble matron of the tribe or town makes choice of anyone she pleases for a Chief. If the person who succeeds is not arrived to years sufficient to take the charge of Government, a regent is appointed, who has the whole authority, but acts in the name of the minor.

The Delewares and Shawanees are remarked for their deceit and perfidy, paying little or no regard to their word and most solemn engagement.

The Tweeghtwees and Yeahtanees are remarkably mild and sedate, and seem to have subdued their passions beyond any other Indians on the continent. They have always been steady friends to the English, and are fond of having them in their country; they might no doubt be made very useful subjects, were proper steps taken to Christianize and civilize them.

The Cherokees are governed by several Sachems or Chiefs (sometimes like the United Provinces or States of Holland) which are elected by their different tribes or villages. The Creeks and Chickasaws have a King and a Council for his assistance, and are esteemed a brave people; they are generally at war with all the other Indians east of the Mississippi; the Chictaws, Creeks, and Cherokees, and those Southern Indians, often fight pitched battles with them on the plains of their country; having horses in plenty, they ride to the field of battle, and there dismount, where the women fight as well as the men, if they are hardly pushed.

CUSTOMS, MANNERS, &c of the I N D I A N S   171

It is supposed that the Chickasaws came from South America, and introduced horses into the North. The Creeks and Chictaws punish their women when they prove disloyal to their husbands, by cutting off their hair, which they will not suffer to grow again till the corn is ripe the next season. The Chickasaws, their neighbors, are not at all troubled with a spirit of jealousy, and say it demands a man to suspect a woman's chastity. They are tall, well shaped, and handsome featured, especially their women, far exceeding in beauty of any other nation to the southward; but even these are exceeded by the Huron women upon Lake Erie, who are allowed to be the best shaped and most beautiful savages by the other nations. They dress much neater than any others, and curiously adorn their heads, necks, wrists, &c. notwithstanding which you will seldom find a jealous husband, either among the Hurons or Five Nation Indians.

The men of the Otawawas, or Souties, are lusty, square, and straight limbed. The women short, thick, and but indifferent for beauty, yet their husbands are very prone to be jealous of them; and whenever this whim comes in their heads, they cut off the tip of the suspected wife's nose, that she may forever after be distinguished by a mark of infamy.

The Indians on the lakes are generally at peace with one another, having a wide extended and fruitful country in their possession. They are formed into a sort of empire, and the Emperor is elected from the eldest tribe, which is the Ottawawas, some of whom inhabit near our fort at Detroit, but are mostly further westward towards the Mississippi. Pontiac is their perfect King or Emperor, who has certainly the largest empire and greatest authority of any Indian Chief that has appeared on the continent since our acquaintance with it. He puts on an air of majesty and princely grandeur, and is greatly honored and revered by his subjects. He not being long formed a design of uniting all the Indian nations together under his authority, but miscarried in the attempt.

In the year 1760, when I commanded and marched the first detachment into this country that was ever sent there by the English, I was met in my way by an embassy from him, of some of his warriors, and some of the chiefs of the tribes that are under him; the purport of which was, to let me know that Pontiac was at a small distance, coming peaceably, and that he desired me to halt my detachment till such time as he could see me with his own eyes. His ambassadors had orders to inform me, that he was Pontiac, the King and Lord of the country I was in.

At first salutation when we met, he demanded my business into his country, and how it happened that I dared to enter it without his leave? When I informed him that it was not with any design against the Indians that I came, but to remove the French out of this country, who had been an obstacle in our way to mutual peace and commerce, and acquainted him with my instructions for that purpose. I, at the same time, delivered him several friendly messages, or belts of wampum, which he received, but gave me no other answer, than that he stood in the path I traveled in till next morning, giving me a small string of wampum, as much as to say, I must not march further without his leave. When he departed for the night, he enquired weather I wanted anything that his country afforded, and he would send his warrior to fetch it? I assured him that any provisions they brought should be paid for; and the next day we were supplied by them with several bags of parched corn, and some other necessaries, At our second meeting he gave me the pipe of peace, and both of us by turns smoked with it; and he assured me he had made peace with me and my detachment; that I might pass thro' his country unmolested; and relieve the French garrison; and that he would protect me and my party from any insults that might be offered or intended by the Indians; and, as an earnest of his friendship, he sent 100 warriors to protect and assist us in driving 100 fat cattle, which we had brought for the use of the Presque Isle. He likewise sent to the several Indian

CUSTOMS, MANNERS, &c of the I N D I A N S 173

towns on the south side and west end of Lake Erie, to inform them that I had his consent to come into the country. He attended me constantly after this interview till I arrived at Detroit, and while I remained in the country, and was the means of preserving the detachment from the fury of the Indians, who had assembled at the mouth of the strait with an intent to cut us off.

I had several conferences with him, in which he discovered great strength of judgment and a thirst after knowledge. He endeavored to inform himself of our military order and discipline. He often intimated to me, that he could be content to reign in his country in subordination to the King of Great Britain, and was willing to pay him such annual acknowledgment as he was able in furs, and to call him his uncle. He was curious to know our methods of manufacturing cloth, iron, &c. and expressed a great desire to see England, and offered me a part of his country if I would conduct him there. He assured me, that he was inclined to live peaceably with the English while they used him as he deserved, and to encourage their settling in his country; but intimated, that, if they treated him with neglect, he would shut up the way, and exclude them from it; in short, his whole conversation sufficiently indicated that he was far from considering himself as a conquered Prince, and that he expected to be treated with the respect and honor the King or Emperor, by all who came into his country, or treated with him.

In 1763, this Indian had the art and address to draw a number of tribes into the English forts upon the lakes, and then make a peace to his mind, by which he intended to establish himself in his Imperial authority; and so wisely were his measures taken, that, in fifteen days time, he reduced or took ten of our garrisons, which were all we had in this country, except Detroit; and had he carried his garrison also, nothing was in the way to obstruct his scheme. Some of the Indians left him, and by his consent made a separate peace; but he would not be active or personally concerned in it, saying when he made a peace, it should be such a one as would be useful and honorable to himself, and to the King of Great Britain; but he has not as yet proposed his terms.

In 1763, when I went to throw provisions into the garrison at Detroit, I sent this Indian a bottle of brandy by a Frenchman. His counselors advised him not to taste it, insinuating that it was poisoned, and sent with a nobleness of mind, laughed at their suspicions, say it was not in my power to kill him, who had so lately saved my life.

In the late war of his, he appointed a commissary, and began to since punctually redeemed. His money was the figure of what he wanted in exchange for it, drawn upon bark, and the shape of an otter (his arms) drawn under it. Were proper measures taken, this Indian might be rendered very serviceable to the British trade and settlements in this country, more extensively so than anyone that hath ever been in alliance with us on the continent.

In traveling northward from Montreal, towards the Ottawawas River, your meet with some few villages belonging to the round Heads, and Ottawawas. The Round Heads are so called from the shape of their heads, there being all possible pains taken by their mothers to make their heads round in their infancy, this being esteemed a great beauty.

On the banks of the river St. Joseph, that flows into Lake Michigan, are two towns settled not long since by the Pottawattamies and Yeahtanees. The Miami Indians were formerly settled upon this river, but are now dispersed into several parts of the country, upon the Miami and the Wabash that empties into the Ohio; the last are known by the name of the Yeahtanees; they are remarkably good-humored and well disposed, and always treat their prisoners with kindness, contrary to the practice of most other Indians.

CUSTOMS, MANNERS, &c of the INDIANS

The language of almost all the Indians to the northward, is undoubtedly derived either from that of the Five Nations or Ottawawas; and any one who is master of these two tongues, may make himself thoroughly understood by upwards of 100 tribes of Indians for though each tribe has some peculiarities in their language, no great difficulty arises there from in conversation.

The Ottawawas, of the two, is understood and spoken by the greatest number. Indeed the Five Nations speak five distinct dialects, tho' they perfectly understand each other.

The Mohawk dialect is the most copious, pathetic, and noble. Their discourses run like a gentle flowing stream, without noise or tumult. Their lips scarcely move through a whole speech. The Ottawawas is spoke quicker, and with greater emotion; but both languages are strong and expressive; and what is more remarkable, they are observed universally to utter themselves with great propriety; a safe syntax, or wrong pronunciation, is seldom known among them. Their language is in many respects very deficient, as they have few words expressive of our abstracted ideas, for before their acquaintance with us they talked about few things that were not present and sensible; so that we were obliged, in order to communicate some of our ideas to them, to make use of numberless circumlocutions, which are tedious and perplexing both to speaker and hearer.

The Indians, especially to the southward, do not neglect to fortify themselves, many of their towns being well stockaded, so as to stand a long siege against an enemy unacquainted with the arts of war. The Five Nations were formerly, accounted the best architects on the continent, and are now inferior to those only near Lake Superior, and some nations to the westward. The Indian houses are generally but the work of half an hour at the most, and sometimes they can range through the woods for months together, without any house at all, or any covering but a skin or blanket.

It is very disagreeable traveling with them, on account of their being enemies to conversation; for they not only never speak themselves but when necessity obliges them, but are displeased with their company if they talk or converse upon a march by land, or a voyage by water.

Among the Chickesaws, Creeks, Cherokees, and others to the southward, you will find a conjuror in almost every village, who pretends to great things, both in politics and physics, understanding to reveal the most hidden secrets, and to tell what passes in the most secret cabinets, and cause the most difficult negotiations to succeed, to procure good fortune to their warriors and hunters, &c. The conjuror, to prepare himself for these exploits, takes a found sweat in a stove, and directly after it plunges into a river or lake, be it ever so cold. But the principal employment of these artist, is the practice of physics and surgery. The Indians have few distempers among them, in comparison of what we have. The gout, gravel, bilious colic, apoplexy, and many other disorders common to us, are unknown to them; nor was the small pox among them till we gave them the infection, since which it hath greatly thinned the numbers of several tribes. They make use of simples in wounds, fractures, dislocations, &c. pouring in the juice or infusion of roots, herbs, &c. into the wound, or into an incision made for the purpose. They likewise make frequent use of bathing, and during the course of the means, the patient has very little nourishment allowed him; and when these simple means (which almost everyone among them knows how to apply) prove ineffectual, the conjuror is called, who exercises his legerdemain over the patient; and whether the patient lives or dies, the worthy doctor is sure to save his credit; for when he sees all hope of recovery past, he never fails to prescribe something that cannot be procured or performed, pretending it to be indispensably necessary, and its efficacy in the present case infallible.

The Indians certainly have remedies that seldom fail in many disorders of their desired effect, particularly in the

CUSTOMS, MANNERS, &c of the INDIANS 177

palsy, dropsy, and the venereal disorder. They frequently make use of cupping and phlebotomy; but their most universal remedy is sweating and the cold bath immediately after it. They often take a sweat by way of refreshment, to compose their minds, and to enable them to speak with greater fluency in public.

They never think a person very dangerously sick till he refuses all kinds of nourishment; and, when this is the case, frequently attribute the disorder to witchcraft, and then the conjuror is sure to be called, who, after sweating, crying, and beating himself, and invoking his genius, confidently assigns the cause of the disorder and a remedy.

The savages who inhabit, or rather wander upon the coasts of Labrador, about the Gulf of St. Lawrence, and the straights of Belle Isle, bear very little resemblance to any of the other Indians in America. They wonder in large parties, are great cowards; their horrid appearance is chief thing to be feared from them; they muffle themselves up in such manner as almost conceals their faces, their shirts terminating in a kind of hood about their head, and at top comes out a tuft of hair that hangs over their foreheads; their coat hangs behind as low as their thighs, and terminates before in a point a little below their girdle; from their girdle hangs a border of trinkets, shells, bones, &c. Their chief clothing are skins and furs, which they put on one over another, to a great number; notwithstanding which heavy dress they appear to be supple and active. They are governed by the old men of each tribe, who form a kind of a senate. Our acquaintance with the Siaux, Nippissongs, and other northern Indians, is yet but very slender; but by the accounts we have, they are idle, savage, cruel, and beastly, beyond any other nations on the continent.

The Seguntacooks, or the Abnaques, settled in New England, were formerly very numerous, as were the Mimaux in Nova Scotia. Of the Penobscots, Narigeewalks, the St. John's Indians, and many other to the eastward and southward of the Gulf of St. Lawrence. There are now scarce any footsteps to be found, except a few families dispersed up and down.

The bark canoes, used by the Indians, seem for their curious workmanship to deserve particular notice. They are made of two kinds of bark, viz. elm and birch. Those made of elm are generally shorter than the others, and not so neatly constructed. The birch canoes are used by the English as well as the Indians upon the island lakes and rivers; they distend the bark, which is very thick, upon a frame of cedar or pine; between the bark and the frame they put small splinters, which help to stiffen and strengthen the canoe. The two ends rise gradually, and terminate in sharp points exactly alike. He that fits behind the steers, and he that is forward looks out to prevent their running foul of anything that might damage the vessel. They sit flat on the bottom, or kneel upon it; their paddles are five or six feet in length, and are in general made of maple. When they go against a current, they use setting poles; but in doing this, great care must be taken to preserve an equilibrium; the canoes being very light, are easily overset. The Bark ribs and bars are sewed together with spruce or pine roots, split to a suitable size, which are more pliant, and do not dry so quick as the elm bark. All the seams are besmeared with gum, inside and out, and every day they examine them. A large canoe will carry twelve men, and some of them more. Among all the savages the Ottawawas are the best builders.

The Indians, in the months of February and March, extract the juice from the maple tree, which is wholesome and delicious to the palate. The way they extract it is by cutting a notch in the body of the tree, and by means of a piece of wood or quill, convey the juice from the tree may be tapped for several years successively. The liquor is as clear as spring water, and is very refreshing. It is accounted a very good pectoral, and was never known to hurt anyone, tho' he drank ever so freely of it. This liquor will not freeze, but when kept any time, becomes excellent vinegar. The

CUSTOMS, MANNERS, &c of the I N D I A N S 179

Indians, by boiling it, make from it a kind of sugar, which has a taste very much like honey, but is milder, and answers all the ends of sugar for sweetening; and, no doubt, was it properly manufactured, might be rendered equal to that extracted from sugar cane. A manufactory of this kind is begun in the Province of New York, near South Bay, which I am told answers very well, and produces considerable quantities of powder and loaf sugar.

There have been many conjectures concerning the different nations of Indians in America, as who, what and from whence they are, it being taken for granted that they are emigrants from some other country. But as the Indians are very solicitous and careful to hand down their own story from father to son, perhaps the account they give of themselves is most deserving of credit. The Hurons and Five Nation Indians, and all the other nations to the southward (except the Chickasaws, came from South America since the Spaniards took possession of it. The Indians on the Great Lakes north of the River St. Lawrence, and those between that river and the Bay of Fundy, and quite to Hudson's Bay northward (except the Eskimaux), tell us that they came from northward.

It will perhaps be agreeable to some to subjoin here an account of the most remarkable animals in America, and of the manner in which the savages take them. And among these the Beaver is deserving of the first notice.

This animal was not unknown in Europe before the discovery of America. It is an amphibious quadruped, that continues not long at a time in the water, but yet cannot live without frequently bathing in it. A large beaver will weigh 60 or 70 lb. Their color is different, according to the country they are taken in. To the northward they are quite black, and to the southward they are almost white, and in the country of the Illinois they are almost the color of the deer, and some have been seen of a yellowish or straw color, the less valuable is their fur.

The beaver lives to a great age; the females generally bring forth four young ones at a time. Its jaws are furnished with two cutters and eight grinders; the upper cutter is two inches and a half long, and the lower something longer. The upper jaw projects over the lower one; the head is shaped like the rat, and is small in proportion to the body; its snout is long, its eyes are small and short, and round and shaggy on the outside, but have no hair within. Its fore feet are not more than five or six inches long, the nails are indented, and hollow like a quill; the hind feet are flat, and webbed between the toes like those of a duck; they walk very slow, but swim fast; the tail is shaped like the blade of a paddle, is four inches broad where it joins the body, five or six in the middle, and three at the extremity, about an inch thick, and a foot long; and there is no flesh, fowl, or fish, that is more agreeable to the palate and the stomach than this part of the beaver; it is covered with a scaly skin, the scales being near a quarter of an inch long, and fold over each other like those of a fish.

The musk bags or castor taken from these animals is of great use among druggists, but it is said are not so good in America as in Russia. The Indians also use them in many disorders. They dress themselves in mantles made from their skins, which after they have worn for some time grow more valuable, for the long hair drops off, and the fur remains more fit for the hat makers use than when raw or fresh taken.

The industry, foresight, and good management among these animals is very surprising, and scarcely credible to those who never saw them. When they want to make a settlement, three, four or more assemble together, and first agree, or pitch upon a place where they may have provisions (which is the bark of trees, lilly roots, or grass) and everything necessary for erecting their edifices, which must be surrounded with water; and if there is neither lake nor pond convenient, they make one by stopping the course of some river or brook with a dam. For this end, they cut down

CUSTOMS, MANNERS, &c of the I N D I A N S 181

trees above the place they are resolved to build it; and they always take their measures so well, as to make the tree fall towards the water, that they may have the less distance to roll it when cut to pieces. This done, they float them down to the place appointed, and these pieces they cut bigger or less, longer or shorter, as the case requires. Sometimes they use the trunks of large trees, which they lay flat in the water; at others, they fasten stakes in the bottom of the channel, and then interweave small branches, and fill up the vacancies with clay, mud and moss, in such a manner as render it very tight and secure.

The construction of their houses is no less artful and ingenious; they are generally built upon piles in their ponds at some distance from the shore, but sometimes upon the banks of rivers; their form is round, with a flat roof; the walls are two feet thick, and sometimes more, and they are built of the same materials as their dams; every part is so well finished that no air can possibly enter; about two thirds of the edifice is raised above the water, and in this they lodge, having the floor strewed with spinsters, &c. to render the lodging comfortable, and they are very careful to keep it clean. They have generally three or four different avenues to each house, but all their doors are under water. As fast as they peel off the bark from the billets of wood laid up for their subsistence, they convey them to their dam to strengthen that, or else pile them on the tops of their houses, and fasten them there with mud. You will sometimes find eight or ten beavers in one house, at others, not more than three or four, and be the number what it will they all lodge upon one floor.

These animals are never found unprovided, by a sudden and unexpected approach of winter; all their business is completed by the end of September, and their stores laid in. They lay up provisions in piles near their houses in such a manner that it keeps under the water fit for their use, the but ends being fastened in the mud or clay at the bottom, so that the current cannot carry it away. When the snows melt and rise the stream, they leave their houses, and everyone goes his own way till the season returns for repairing them, or for building new ones, which is the month of July, when they reassemble, or else form new associations. The Ground Beavers, as they are called, conduct their affairs in a different manner; all the care they take is, to make a kind of covered way to the water. They are easily known from the others by their hair, which is much shorter. They are always very poor, the natural consequence of their idleness. The Indians never hunt these but out of necessity.

The manner of hunting beaver is very simple and easy, for this animal has not strength enough to defend itself. The Indians hunt them from November to April, in which season their fur is best. They either decoy them into traps, or shoot them; but the latter is very difficult, by reason of the quickest of their sight and motion; and should they happen to wound them mortally in the water, it is a chance if they ever get them out.

They lay their traps in the paths frequented by the beaver, and bait them with fresh cut poplar boughs, which they are very fond of, and ramble abroad for, notwithstanding their winter store. Sometimes the Indians open the ice near the beaver houses, at which opening one stands, while another disturbs the house; the beaver hastens upon this to make his escape at the opening, and seldom fails of having his rains beat out the moment he raises his head above water.

The beavers which frequent the lakes, besides their houses in the water, have a kind of country house, two or three hundred yards from it, and the Indians here hunt them from one to the other. When these animals discover an enemy of any kind, they hasten into the water, and give warning to their companions, by flapping the water with their tails, which may be heard at a considerable distance.

The Muskrat resembles the beaver in every part, excepting its tail, which is round like a rat's. One of these

CUSTOMS, MANNERS, &c of the I N D I A N S   183

animals weighs about five or six pounds; during the summer season the male and female keep together, but separate at the approach of winter, and each seek a shelter in some hollow tree, without laying up any provision.

Scarce anything among the Indians is undertaken with greater solemnity than hunting the Bear: and an alliance with a noted bear hunter, who has killed several in one day, is more eagerly sought after, than that of one who has rendered himself famous in war; the reason is, because the catch supplies the family with both food and payment. So expert are some of the Indians at passing thro' the woods and thickets, that they run down the bears in autumn when they are fat, and then drove them with switches to their own towns.

The bears lodge, during the winter, either in hollow trees, or caves; they lay up no provision, and have no nourishment during this season, but what they suck from their own claws, yet they retain both their strength and fat without any sensible diminution.

The bear is not naturally fierce, unless when wounded, or oppressed by hunger. They run themselves very poor in the month of July, and it is somewhat dangerous to meet them till this appetite is satisfied, and they recover their flesh, which they do very suddenly. These animals are very fond of grapes, and most kinds of fruit. When provisions are scarce in the woods, they venture out among the settlements, and make great havoc of the Indian corn, and sometimes kill the swine. Their chief weapons are their fore paws, with which they will hug any animal they get into them immediately to death.

The elk is near and large as a horse, but resembles the deer, and, like it, annually renews its horns. The Indians have a great veneration for this animal, and imagine that to dream of it portends good fortune and long life.

The elk delights in cold countries, feeding upon grass in summer, and moss buds, &c. in winter, when they herd together. It is dangerous to approach very near this animal when he is hunted, as he sometimes springs furiously on his pursuers, and tramples them to pieces. To prevent this, the hunter throws his clothes to him, and while the deluded animal spends his fury on these, he takes proper measures to dispatch him.

The catamounts and wild cats are great enemies to the elk, and often make a prey of him. He has no other way to disengage himself from these, but by plunging into the water.

On the south and west parts of the Great Lakes, and both sides of the Mississippi, the most noted is that of the buffalo.

The hunters encompass as large a tract as they can, where they supposed the buffalos are, and so as the fire advances towards the center, they close up nearer and nearer, by which means they generally slaughter all that happen to be thus enclosed. The buffalo is a large heavy animal, has short, thick, crooked, black horns, and a large beard hanging from his muzzle and head, a part of which falls down by his eyes, and gives him a disagreeable appearance; the back is rounded, covered with hair; on the other parts of the body is a kind of wool. Those to the northward about Hudson's Bay have the best wool upon them, and in the greatest abundance.

There are in this country some panthers, which prey upon almost every living thing that comes in their way. Their flesh is white like veal, and agreeable to the palate, and their fur is valuable.

Here are likewise foxes of various colors, black, grey, red, and white, who by their craft and cunning make great havoc among the water fowl by a thousand deceitful capers, which they cut upon the banks of the lakes and rivers.

CUSTOMS, MANNERS, &c of the INDIANS

The skunk or pole-cat is very common, and is called by the Indians the "Stinking Beast", on account of its emitting a disagreeable savor to a considerable distance when pursued or disturbed. It is about the size of a small cat, has shining hair of a grey color, with two white lines, that form an oval, on its back. The fur of this animal, with that of the ermin, otter, and martin, make up what they call the small peltry. The ermin is about the size of the squirrel, its fur is extremely white, its tail long, and the tip of it as black as jet. The martin, or sable, lives principally among the mountains, is as long as a common cat, but very slender; the fur is very fine and valuable.

The opossum is a remarkable animal in this country having under its belly a bag or false belly, in which they breed their young. The young one proceed from the teats to which they stick, as a part thereof, till they take life, and issue forth, or rather drop off. And to this false belly they fly for shelter and protection in case of any alarm.

The porcupine is as large as a small dog. Its quills are about two inches and a half long, white, and hollow, and very strong, especially on its back; they quickly bury themselves, and occasion great pain.

The savages make great use of these quills for ornamenting their clothes, belts arms, &c.

The moose is larger than a large horse, and is one of the deer kind, every year changing his horns; the color of this animal is a dark brown, the hair coarse. He has a mane like a horse, a dulap like a cow, a very large head, and a short tail. During the summer he frequents bogs and swamps; in the winter, the north sides of the hills and mountains, where the sun will not melt the snow. Their common pace of traveling is a trot, but hunted are very swift.

It hath been sufficiently remarked, as we have traveled through this extensive country, that it everywhere abounds with fish, fowl, and variety of game, that in its forests are most kinds of useful timber, and a variety of wild fruit might be cultivated and raised here in great perfection. In a word, this country wants nothing but that culture and improvement, which can only be the effect of the time and industry, to render it equal, if not superior, to any in the world.

F I N I S

Robert Rogers

Appendix

Robert Rogers was born in Methuen, Massachusetts on November 7, 1731, to James Jacob Rogers and Mary Mc Fatridge. In the spring of 1739 his father moved the Family to the Township of Dunbarton, New Hampshire. In 1748 his family farm was burned by raiding Indians and the family took shelter in Rumford now Concord He led Rogers' Rangers in the French and Indian War 1755 to 1763 also known as the Seven Years War. Around 1755 Robert survived a bout with small pox which soon afterwards in 1757 took the life of his brother Richard. Robert married Elizabeth Browne around 1760. He had one known child with Elizabeth named Arthur Rogers who was born on February 12, 1769. General John Stark served under Rogers as a Lieutenant in Rogers' Rangers.

Major Robert Rogers returned to New England and when the American Revolution broke out, John Stark tried to convince George Washington to let Rogers join the provincials, but Washington believed that Rogers was a British spy and refused to let him enter the camp. Major Robert Rogers was then made Colonel in the Kings Rangers, which must have troubled him to be fighting against his fellow colonists, causing him to return to England rather than fight his friends. He was divorced from Elizabeth in 1778 and she remarried John Roche. He died on May 18, 1795 and was said to be buried in a Church yard which later became the Elephant Hotel and Castle, in Borough, England.

Much of the following is from a letter written by Walter James Rogers Esq. and read to Canada's Parliament by his father Colonel Henry. Cassedy Rogers on December 14th 1899.

Colonel H. C. Rogers (center and inset) Queen's Rangers 1899

Robert had three brothers in Rogers' Rangers, they were Captain Richard Rogers, his little brother John also is listed as a recruit in 1757 and may have stayed in the south after their 1762 visit to Charleston. Colonel James Rogers, who was commandant of the King's Rangers for five years, during the American Revolution, his Rangers formed part of the garrison of St Johns, Quebec. This post commanded the northern outlet of the great waterway which connects the Valley of the Hudson with that of the St. Lawrence. At the peace in 1784, James settled with some two hundred of his disbanded soldiers upon the shores of the Bay of Quinte, he and his followers occupying what is known as the township of Fredericksburg, as well as part of an adjoining Township of Adolphustown.

In the Seven Years War, James Rogers was a captain in command of a detachment and served, independently of the Robert Rogers' main regiment of Rangers, he took part in the campaigns in Cape Breton and Canada, under Wolfe and Amherst. He was present at the successive captures of

APPENDIX 189

Louisburg, Quebec, and Montreal; the steps by which Canada passed from French to English rule before Montreal, the main body of the Rogers' Rangers, eight hundred strong, under the command of Robert Rogers, had played a somewhat conspicuous part. Upon the capitulation of Montreal and the cession of Canada, this latter officer was dispatched by the commander-in-chief upon the first British expedition, as such, up the Great lakes. With two hundred of his Rangers and a staff of executive officers, Robert Rogers made the voyage, in whaleboats, from Montreal to Detroit. The successive French posts upon the route were visited; the white standard of the Bourbons was replaced by the flag of Great Britain, and allegiance to His Britannic Majesty exacted.

The story of this voyage has often been told, notably in the Major's own military journals published in London in 1765; a work, which, with its companion volume, 'A Concise Account of North America', which he had an intimate knowledge of the continent from Labrador to the mouth of the Mississippi has ever since been regarded as a valuable authority upon the geographical history of this country.

With the early and more brilliant part of the career of Robert Rogers, who's exploits as a Partisan or light-infantry officer fill a large space in the history of the French and Pontiac Wars, we are not here immediately concerned. He has been the object of enthusiastic praise and of no less virulent detraction. It is, however, a source of what, I trust, you will not regard as altogether unpardonable pride to my, family and myself, that one of our name should have been thus intimately concerned in a transaction which was virtually the inception, as part of the British Dominions, of what is now the Province of Ontario, a province which, from its earliest settlement, has been our home.

Between the close of the French and Indian Wars, and until after the outbreak of the American Revolution, Robert Rogers spent most of his time in England. Here his various books were published and here he enjoyed a very considerable notoriety. In old magazines of the period, chronicles of the time, his exploits and his books find frequent mention. The story of his prowess in the single-handed capture of a highwayman went the round of the taverns. His portrait in full Ranger uniform, with Indians in the background, adorned the windows of the print shops, and was even reproduced in Germany. His tall figure, in half-pay officer's uniform, became a not unfamiliar object in the Court quarter of the town. He undoubtedly enjoyed the patronage and favor of the King. One of his enemies writing in 1770 to Sir William Johnson complains that "Robert Rogers has the ear of the court; that many of the great are pushing for him; and that Mr. Fitz Herbert, an officer high in the household of George III, is his particular friend". Indeed, to the end he seems to have enjoyed the not entirely unequivocal distinction of King George's approbation. Lord George Germaine, writing to Gen. Howe as late as 1776, says, "The King approves the arrangement you propose, in respect to an adjutant-general, and a quartermaster-general, and also your attention to Major Rogers, of who's firmness and fidelity we have received further testimony from Governor Tryon."

George III's choice of instruments at this period, notably in the case of Lord George himself, as Secretary for the Colonies, is not generally regarded as betraying exceptional political sagacity.

Notwithstanding the royal favor, which does not seem to have been alienated even by his alleged eccentricity in appearing for a wager, on one occasion, at the King's levee, in the buckskin gaiters worn by Rangers during their woodland campaigns, Robert Rogers was probably more at home in the society of soldiers of fortune, where his prowess as a boon companion and raconteur was doubtless popular.

In 1772 we find him writing from his lodgings at Spring Gardens, Charing Cross, Soon after that, his superfluous energies found vent in foreign warfare. A true Captain Dalgetty, he fought in Northern Africa in the Algerian service. We know from a letter of Washington's that he was assigned to service in the East Indies when the outbreak of hostilities in America recalled him to the scene of his earlier activities. That he arrived in America with an open mind is not impossible. Unlike his less brilliant but more substantial brother, James, he was probably not the man to suffer gladly for a principle.

The conduct of the rebels, however, forced him prematurely into the service which would, probably, in any event have ultimately claimed him. Arrested shortly after his landing at Philadelphia, by order of the Pennsylvania Committee of Public Safety, he was submitted to the disposal of Congress. This body ordered his release on parole. His position as a half-pay officer, however, and his long identification with the royal service attracted the suspicion of the more violent whips, who clamored for his re-arrest, which was ultimately decided upon. The indignity of this second arrest was treated by him as a virtual release from his parole. Consigned by the Continental Congress as a prisoner to be dealt with by the New Hampshire Assembly, he was fortunate enough to effect his escape. Received within the English lines, he was offered by the commander-in-chief, General Howe, the commission of colonel in the British service, which offer he accepted.

With remarkable celerity he succeeded raising the regiment so honorably known in the history of the revolution as the Queen's Rangers. This corps, to which very frequent reference has been made in the transactions of this Society played, under his successor in the command, Colonel, afterwards Lieutenant-General Simcoe, a conspicuous part in the war, and subsequently, in the settlement of Upper Canada. Broken in health and possibly enfeebled by a life of dissipation, a tendency to which seems to have been his real moral weakness, he retired from his command in the following winter and returned to England. The evil example of dissipation and high play set at the headquarters camp between Bedford and Amboy, in the winter of 1776-77 was not without its effect upon the morale of the army. Bancroft even attributes the failure to crush Washington at Valley Forge in the following winter, to the eager-pursuit of pleasure which distinguished Howe's command. Meanwhile the Revolution ran its course, The singular incapacity which marked the conduct of the English arms almost throughout, was responsible for reverse after reverse. Spasmodic efforts to reinforce the army in America were made, and as the result of one of these, Robert Rogers arrived at New York in 1779 with instructions from home that he was to be again employed.

On May 1, 1779, he was commissioned by Sir Henry Clinton, Howe's successor in the command-in-chief, to raise a regiment of two battalions to be known as the King's Rangers. One battalion seems to have been destined for service In the Province of Quebec; the other for Halifax. In this regiment his brother James was gazetted major. A document in the War Office Correspondence shows that James Roger's appointment dated June 2, 1779, although there as a still earlier commission to the same rank dated May 1, 1778. Recruiting parties were sent out into the northern colonies and a ship was chartered by government for the conveyance to Quebec of Major James Rogers and eleven officers gazetted to the new corps. This vessel, the brigantine Hawk," Capt Slaitor, arrived at Quebec in September 1779. The colonel, Robert Rogers, with a staff of officers, was conveyed in H.M.S. "Blond" to Penobscot. There he was present at the naval engagement in which the rebel fleet was destroyed August 13, 1779.

Meanwhile, with the accustomed mismanagement at headquarters, no definite instructions were sent to General Haldimand, Commander-in-chief in Canada, as to the embodiment of the new corps. So early as May 24th 1779 Lord Rawdon, afterwards Lord Hastings, Governor General

APPENDIX 193

of India, then acting as Adjutant General to Clinton' wrote to Haldimand, indicating the probable appearance of Col. Robert Rogers within the latter's command. With official dread of exceeding his instructions, and fearful of provoking animosities regarding recruiting in the other corps in the province, Haldimand hesitated how to act.

Meanwhile, the numerous recruits coming in by the overland route, consigned to the King's Rangers, had to be subsisted as best they might out of the unfortunate major's own pocket. Ultimately, however, and upon his own authority, Haldimand placed the corps upon his own establishment. A scale of half-pay was arranged, and the Rangers were clothed in the regulation green uniforms of the provincial corps. From this time forward the King's Rangers garrisoned the post of St. Johns, sharing the barracks there at first with the 34th and, subsequently, with the 29th regiments of foot.

The correspondence of James Rogers with the commander-in-chief in Canada, from 1779 to 1784, is still preserved in the British Museum, and together with furitive letters of Robert Rogers, fills a substantial folio volume of manuscript. The "Field Officers Letters of Rogers' King's Rangers" are in the Record Office, London, removed there from the War Office Archives. The light which these old documents throw upon the military history of the time is a curious one. The chief difficulties in the administration of the corps seem to have arisen concerning the matter of recruiting and the intermingling of the accounts with those of Halifax, where the other detachment of the regiment was stationed. For the rest, James Roger's relations with his commander-in-chief are excellent. Repeated testimony to the confidence felt in his integrity at headquarters occurs in the correspondence. His long apprenticeship to warfare, his intimate knowledge of the country, and undoubted zeal for the King's service contributed to his usefulness at this frontier post. Various schemes of reconnaissance and attack were, from time to time, submitted by him for his

Excellency's consideration, and approved. His advice is asked and taken. On more than one occasion he seems to have been employed, where a field officer's services were demanded, upon missions of delicacy and importance. The growing despondency as to the issue of the war is apparent as time goes on. Incredulity as to the truth of the surrender at Yorktown succeeded by consternation when the news of tile disaster is confirmed. At last, in November 1781, the King's order for the disbanding of the loyalist troops arrives. It is accompanied by extracts from Lord North's letters respecting the allotment of lands to the provincial troops and refugee loyalists then in the Province of Quebec.

Throughout the winter of 1783-84, preparations are made for the move westward in the following year In the early spring, my great-great-grandfather paid that last visit to his former home, allusion to which has been made above. His wife, a daughter of the Rev. David McGregor of Londonderry, New Hampshire, accompanied him. on his return, to renew in the northern forests that life of exile which had been the lot of her family earlier in the century. Upon his return to St. Johns, leave is asked on behalf of a number of incorporated and unincorporated loyalists, that an officer of the King's Rangers and a detachment of ten or a dozen men may go to Cataraqui to reconnoitre. A pathetic touch, betraying the ignorance and bewilderment of those distracted times, occurs, where the commanding officer notifies the commander-in-chief of a report which he had come upon "amongst our common men, that the major was going to have them taken to Cataraqui and there made slaves. Notwithstanding this alarming suggestion, confidence seems to have been restored; and most of the King's Rangers accompanied their old commander in that heroic advance into the wilderness, in search of a new home. Several of the officers remained at St. Johns, buying the ground on which their late barracks stood.

The tale of how the final allotment of the territory in the Frontenac district was made is set out in Grass's narrative preserved by Dr. Ryerson. Grass, the pioneer of the district, chose the first township for his followers, Kingston; Sip John Johnson, the second, Ernesttown; Col Rogers, the third, Fredericksburg; Major Vanalstine, the fourth', Adolphustown; and Col. McDonell and his company, the fifth, Marysburgh; "and so after this manner the first settlement of loyalists in Canada was made."

In the pages of Canniffs work upon the "Settlement of Upper Canada" is preserved a story told by the late Dr. Armstrong, whose recollections dated back to the closing years of the eighteenth century. He remembered to have seen as a child, at my great-great-grandfather's house at Fredericksburg, a quantity of old implements of war: broken firelocks, torn uniforms, and cannonballs. Not a few relics of the soldier settlement still exist in the family, in the shape of rusty small-arms, obsolete powder-horns and flint lock pistols.

Is Robert buried in New Hampshire? Some say no, I say prove it.

In the Greenfield Village Cemetery in Greenfield, New Hampshire is the grave of a Robert Rogers who died December 30th, 1808 in his 79th year at the bottom of his tombstone reads "Death Thou hast conquer'd me I by thy darts am slain But Christ has conquer'd thee And I shall rise again" I was led to this site from a Boston Globe article that Ranger Pat Keon, of Dunbarton gave me which reported a descendant of Robert's, Mrs. John N. Bryer stated that this was the grave of Major Robert Rogers, who had returned to New Hampshire and married a second wife Sarah Alexander. He had lived in Greenfield in seclusion to avoid troubles from his previous marriage and his expulsion from New Hampshire.

Robert did express a wish to return to New Hampshire and he was a good friend of General Stark. There are surnames of other Rogers' Rangers in the cemetery who may have aided and helped conceal him in Greenfield which is a halfway point between Londonderry and Fort #4. He did not show up here until after his he was last seen in London. The age of 79 on this grave would place his birth at about 1729 which is within the reported dates of Robert's birth which vary from 1728 to 1731. It could be the 1731 date may actually be the date of his christening.

I have been told by other Rogers researchers that they have been told by historians that this is not Major Robert Rogers, but they have not given me the names of the historians they consulted nor any facts to back up their claim. They have no information on where this Robert Rogers came from, who his parents were or any background on him.

I believe that if Robert did return to his loved America that this is his grave. If anybody has concrete proof that it is not, please present it. If this is Robert an exhumation would provide definitive proof, based on his injuries to his left wrist, head and other battle wounds. The DNA could be compared with living and deceased descendants.

In Memory of Mr.
ROBERT ROGERS
who died
Dec 30, 1808 in the
79 years of his age
Death Thou hast conquer'd me
I by thy darts am slain
But Christ has conquer'd thee
And I shall rise again

198   A CONCISE ACCOUNT OF NORTH AMERICA

Grave of Robert Rogers in Greenfield, New Hampshire.

Statue of Major Robert Rogers on Rogers Island, Fort Edward, New York. Sculpted by Alice Manzi and dedicated on May 30, 2005.

APPENDIX 199

I have made spelling and name changes from the original 18th century English to modern English. The lower case letter "s" when in the beginning or middle of a word was whaqt is called a script s and looked more like a half crossed f like this " ſ " and at the end of a word it was "s". Hence "Mississippi" was "Miffiffippi", "case" was "cafe" and "Missouri" was "Mifauris", Atlantic was Atlantick, Business was Bufinefs, false was falfe, Panama was the Isthmus of Darien, Pacific was Pacifick, shall was fhall, sheep was fheep, some was fome, such was fuch, subject was fubject etc. etc.

Anticosti was Anticosta
Appalachian was Aplalachian
Choose was chuse
Dalhousie was Thoulouse
Appalachian was Apalachain
Chesapeake was Chesepeak
Britannic was Britannick
Hartford was Hertford
Kennebec, was Kennebeck,
Maine was Main
Massachusetts was Massachuset's
Miami was Miamee
Michigan was Mechigan
Mohawk was Mohock
Oneida was Oineyda
Onondaga was Onondago
Passaic was Passaick
Pennsylvania was Pensylvania
Pocahontas was Pocahantas
Pontiac was Ponteak
Rappahannock River was Rappahanock River
Roanoke was Ronoak
Schenectady was Shenectady
Shippensburg was Shippesburg
Staten Island was Streighten Island

Susquehanna was Susquahanah

APPENDIX

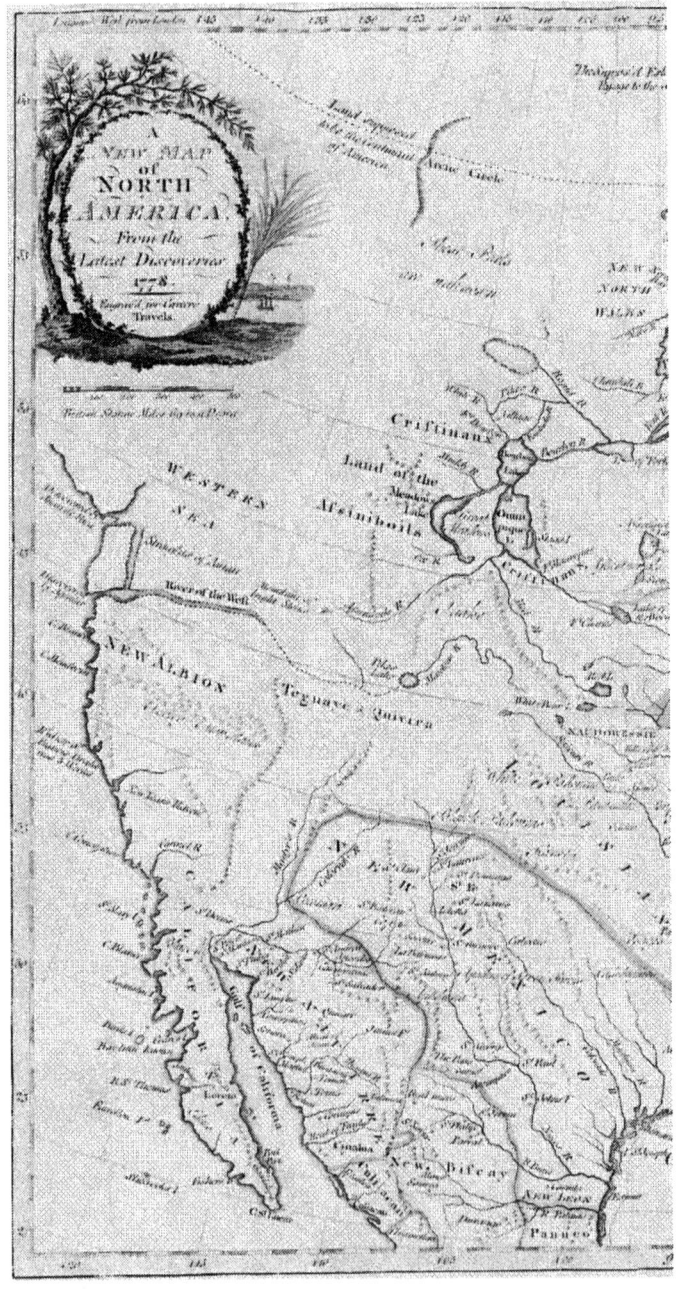

APPENDIX

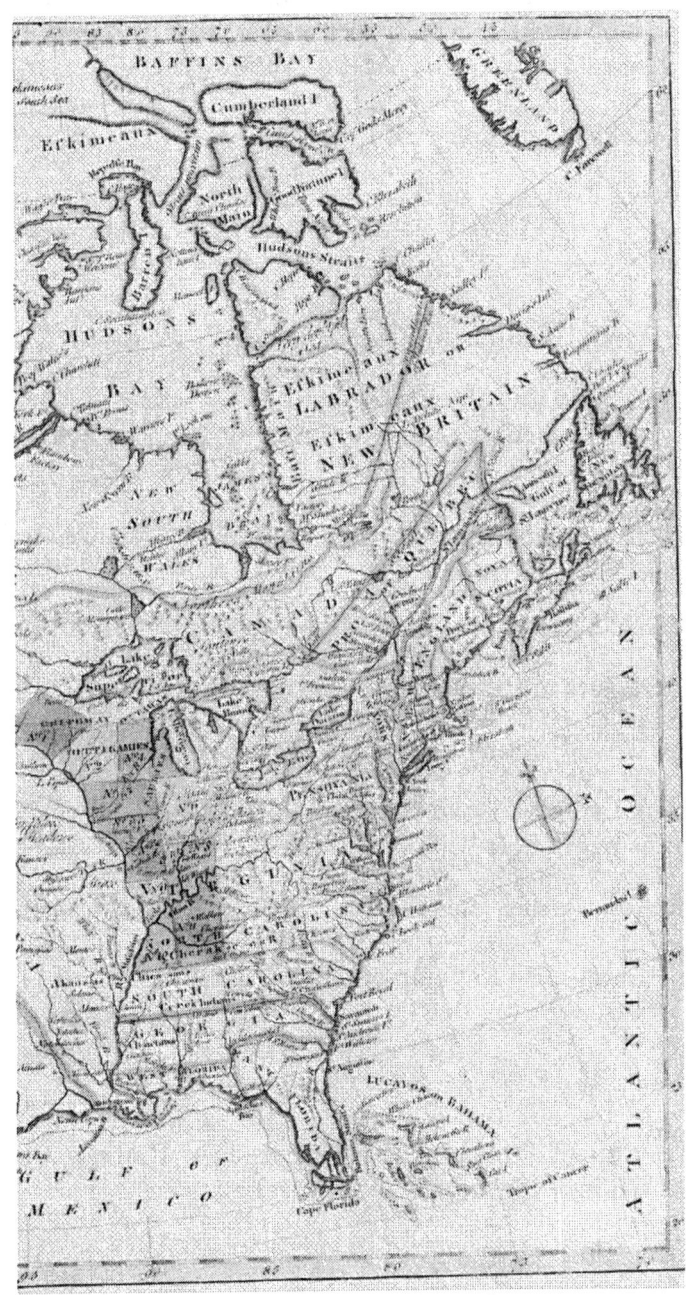

The previous page contains a 1775 map made by John Carver, who was Roberts Rogers' map maker and part of the party Rogers had sent to find the Northwest Passage.

Other books about Robert Rogers

Northwest Passage. By Kenneth Roberts.

A True Ranger. By Gary Zaboly.

White Devil, By Stephen Brumwell.

The Annotated and Illustrated Journals of Major Robert Rogers. Introduction and Annotation by Timothy J. Todish. Illustrated by Gary S. Zaboly.

Reminiscence of the French War. By: Robert Rogers and General Stark.

Crucible of War. By: Fred Anderson's.

Robert Rogers of the Rangers. By: John R. Cuneo

Rising Above Circumstances. By: Robert J. Rogers.

The Impossible Major Rogers, By: Patricia Lee Gauch, drawings by: Robert Andrew Parker

Warfare on the Colonial Frontier, By: Robert Rogers.

Scalp Hunters, By Raymond G. Potvin & Alfred E. Kayworth.

Internet

Descendants of James Rogers, Father of the Rangers web site by William Gorman www.Montalona.com

APPENDIX

About William M. Gorman

Descended from Robert Rogers' brother, Colonel James Rogers born 1726, his son James Rogers born 1764, his son David Rogers born 1805, his daughter Mary Allen Rogers born 1845, her son Robert D. Gorman born 1876, his son Leland W. Gorman born 1906 and his son Robert W. Gorman born 1932. All of them are gone now and all were very proud to be related to the famous James and Robert Rogers of Rogers' Rangers.

I got involved in researching my family's history to complete the research started by my late mother, Arlene, who in 1972, took my siblings and I on a cross country trip looking up records and searching graveyards for ancestors. Since then I have made a tremendous addition to her efforts. Sadly her ancestors have been very difficult to trace. We visited Sandhurst, Ontario where a Historical marker for Colonel James Rogers stands. I believe the marker, the church and grave yard are on lot 7 where James lived and his grave is here but missing the head stone. The Rogers side of the family is on my father's side, he is also descended from the Hopkins of the Mayflower and the Jones family that arrived with Captain Smith in Virginia. Aside from my native American ancestors, next year will be the 400th anniversary of my ancestors immigration to America.

On page 12 my 10th Great Grandfather Major General Robert Sedgwick is mentioned, he took Port Royal in 1654. Through James Rogers' wife Margaret McGregor, daughter of Rev. David McGregor, her brother, Robert built the first bridge over the Merrimack River and her sister Mary is the grandmother of Jane Means Appleton, wife of President Franklin Pierce. Other famous ancestors include Captain James Avery of Groton, Connecticut of which Avery point is named for. Samuel L. Clemmons is a 3rd cousin. My families linage includes over 100 King, 100 Queens and hundreds of princes and princesses of every Kingdom in Europe. Lady Godiva is also an ancestor, turns out she was likely in her 60's or 70's when she made her ride, she was born about 980 and the ride was in the second half of the eleventh century.

My 4th Great Grandfather, James Rogers III married Mary Allen born in 1775, who may be the daughter of Ethan Allen. I believe after Ethan's death her step-mother, Fanny, in her greed wrote her off as dead for marring a loyalist who owned close to 50,000 acres. Fanny did this to prevent Mary from inheriting any of her fathers lands.

I am currently living in Manchester, New Hampshire and am a member of the Dunbarton Historical Society, where the Rogers family lived in the mid 1700's. We are trying to get a state historical marker for the site of the Rogers home where Robert grew up. I work full time and in my spare time maintain the Descendants of James Rogers web site at Montalona.com and work on family related book projects.

www.ingramcontent.com/pod-product-compliance
Lightning Source LLC
Chambersburg PA
CBHW050145170426
43197CB00011B/1966